A'undressing the **Judge**

A'undressing the **Judge**

HE COULD HAVE EVERYTHING—
BUT NOT HER SON

JC PARRY

authorHOUSE®

AuthorHouse™
1663 Liberty Drive
Bloomington, IN 47403
www.authorhouse.com
Phone: 1-800-839-8640

Published by AuthorHouse   11/12/2012

ISBN: 978-1-4772-3853-0 (sc)
ISBN: 978-1-4772-3854-7 (e)

Contents

Foreword

To my beloved husband for all his love and support

For my sons

With my love

Preface

Joanne and Chris had flown to Barcelona to attend a medical conference, it had been three long days of meetings and speeches and now, at nine in the evening it was time to relax.

Joanne was pleased with the hotel; it appeared to match the description in the brochure and was an impressive building, large and modern, with white stonewalls in the Moorish style. There were four grand pillars at the entrance and the footmen in uniform stationed by the blue glass doors had been eager to help them with their bags.

Their hotel room was softly lit; the main focus was the dark carved mahogany bed with its rich coloured bedspread that made a pleasing contrast to the crisp white sheets and huge white pillows arranged against the bed-head.

Exhausted, Joanne and Chris snuggled up together in the generous bed and flicked through the list of films available to watch on the hotel TV. They decided to choose the film 'North Country', a story about a girl's struggle to expose the truth.

Chris' tall body was, as usual, a bit too long for the bed and Joanne could see his toes stuck out from under the sheets. She enjoyed the feel of his warm body next to her. She loved to touch him, he felt so strong and fit and she loved the clean warm smell of his skin. She watched the light from the TV flicker over his face and highlight his features. Chris, aware of her gaze, turned and kissed her affectionately, his fair hair swept back from his face, emphasising his beautiful grey eyes. Joanne thought how nice it was to have some time alone together, it made her feel romantic and she adjusted her long blond hair over her shoulders and snuggled up even closer.

It was quiet. The only sound came from the TV and Joanne drifted into thought. Maybe she should expose what really went on behind those great walls of so-called English *Justice*[1]. Now that their ordeal was over, it was easy to push the memories to the back of her mind and just get on with life; even pretend it never happened. But watching the movie made Joanne think again. If she didn't reveal what happened, it would mean that some Judges could continue to misinterpret the law for their own end and CAFCASS[2] cases such as theirs would be remain buried in the bowels of the Court archives.

---

[1] English Justice: The Court's duty, according to the Children Act 1989 was to ascertain the wishes and feelings of the child; his physical, emotional and educational needs; any harm that he is suffering or is likely to suffer and the capability of any parent to meet the child's needs.

[2] CAFCASS: The Children and Family Court Advisory and Support Service; is independent of the Courts, Social Services and other similar authorities. It was set up in 2001 to look after the interests of children and then advise the Courts on what it considers to be in the best interests of the child, bearing in mind the child's wishes and feelings, his physical, emotional and educational needs.

Chapter One

The Year 2003

Joanne's memories of 2003 came drifting back to her. It was four years ago in the summer when the story hit the headlines. Joanne was in the gym to do a workout. She wore her white T-shirt with its pink edging and shorts to match. She didn't much like the gym because there were no windows to look outside; it seemed shut off from the world. The room was lit with bright fluorescent lights and the air conditioning made it feel cool, but not really fresh. It was pretty crowded that day with people on monotonous exercise machines, mindlessly wired to their iPods. Large TV screens surrounded the walls for entertainment and Joanne thought how she preferred to be outdoors in the fresh-air. If she were going to exercise she would rather be going somewhere, cycling, walking, running. She liked to feel her long hair, soft on her back, swish to and fro as she ran. But that summer day was incredibly hot and the only place to exercise was inside in the gym.

She remembered the TV screens had suddenly caught her attention. Instead of the endless stream of advertisements, she saw pictures of herself and Sam. Joanne stared in amazement. There they were, pictures of her, on Sky News; and their story flashed up on all the screens. It was like a dream, but yes, it was real. Their story was out there, for the entire world to see.

Later, back home, she opened the front door and was enthusiastically greeted by Springer. Not exactly the most original name for a Springer Spaniel, but it was Sam's dog and that was what he wanted to call him. Lying on the doormat Joanne saw that neighbours had pushed newspaper cuttings through the letterbox. There were articles from The Times, The Guardian and The Telegraph; they too had got hold of the story.

Joanne walked into the living room and switched on the TV. She keyed in the remote control for BBC News 24 and stood there in anticipation. Yes, sure enough, there was the picture of the front page of The Sun.

The serious grey haired newsreader in his dark BBC suit held up the front page of the paper for viewers to see. He pointed to a picture of Joanne and Sam, their faces pixillated-out to disguise their identity and of course it was not their real names that were printed there.

What a cop-out! Thought Joanne, if a Court Order involved a child, it was illegal to identify the child in public. Judges could make any Court Order they wished and the public would never know about it, never be able to criticise how the case had been handled.

Joanne was fascinated at the way the BBC had presented this story. The newsreader turned to interview a solicitor who sat next to him. The pretty city lawyer must have been asked to come into the BBC studios at short notice to be made up, camera ready, to comment on the case. She was dressed in a smart grey suit with a pink silk scarf around her neck to give a bit of colour, her short dark hair swept back off her face. She seemed rather stressed and the interview became more like an interrogation.

"How is it that this child was allowed to suffer so much in the hands of the Courts and for so many years? *Ten years* of going through the Courts. In total, *eighty* Court cases. *Ten years* of this little boy's life spent going through all those Court hearings."

The newsreader pulled the paper closer to be able to read directly from the page and he continued:

"I quote Sam; who says here in his own words that he has lost his childhood, that someone ought to get it back for him and all he ever wanted to do was get on with his life".

The solicitor looked put on the spot, but the BBC newsreader persisted;

"Is this law a *bad* law?" he demanded, "Should it not be *changed*?"

There was a pause as the solicitor considered how best to answer his question. She had to be careful. She was a partner in a well-known law company and she represented the family division of that company. The other high profile cases that the company had handled were mostly for the stars and their notable divorce cases. She knew she must not upset the Judiciary and must not let down her company. Yet, as a woman, maybe she could see it from another point of view.

Finally, the solicitor responded,

"Its not a *bad* law. It was just *badly interpreted*!"

φ

Now that their story was in the newspapers, Joanne realised that she would have to be vigilant. She could be prosecuted for leaking the story to the papers. She turned off the TV and called her parents and warned them not to say anything to friends or neighbours. She told them that it was probably best not to keep any copies of the newspapers, or anything that could connect Joanne to the story.

Then Joanne looked at her watch and realised that it was time to go and collect Alex from school. Sam was old enough at thirteen to walk to and from school, but Alex was only eight and he still needed someone to pick him up. Joanne quickly put a lead on Springer, locked the door behind her and, with Springer straining at his collar, they started the short walk to Alex's school. The afternoon sun was still warm on Joanne's back and she began to feel lighter, even elated. Bit by bit, she began to appreciate that, after all this time, at last the case was over. She wondered if the headmistress had seen the newspapers.

At the gates of the school Joanne keyed in the security code and entered the narrow hallway that doubled as a cloakroom, with coats and bags hanging untidily on pegs. The cloakroom door then led into the large main assembly hall where the headmistress sat opposite the entrance. All the classrooms were off this main hall and it allowed the headmistress to keep an eye on both pupils and staff as they came and went. Joanne walked into the assembly hall and approached the headmistress's desk. She looked up and greeted Joanne with a welcoming smile.

"Congratulations! You made it into the headlines! It was on Sky news too, did you see it?"

"Yes. Thank you. You know you've been such a tremendous support. I don't know how we would have managed without your help with the school fees. I felt so guilty, Chris having spent all his earnings on solicitor's fees and even though I mostly acted alone in Court, we needed solicitor's advice of how to go about it. And, we wouldn't have won Sam's freedom without the QC. In the end it took a *QC* to get the Judge to listen!"

The headmistress looked kindly at Joanne,

"I understood how you felt, that is why I wanted to help you both."

At that moment one of the classroom doors opened. It was Alex's teacher. She had the children lined-up crocodile fashion ready to be collected and then the noise in the hall increased as other mothers entered the hall to take their charges home. Alex was released from his class line-up. He rushed straight up to Joanne and flung his arms around her. His teacher motioned to the other pupils to remain in line and she came over to speak to Joanne.

"Was that you, was that *really you and Sam* on the front page?" she asked excitedly.

The headmistress motioned her to keep her voice down and shook her head disapprovingly.

"Discretion is paramount. We mustn't talk about it!"

The teacher nodded, she understood. She smiled and turned back to rejoin her pupils.

As Joanne walked home with Alex, his small hand in hers, he chatted away about his day, while

Springer fussed about his legs with excitement. Alex always chatted so much there wasn't really any need for her to speak, other than to make the occasional acknowledgment. Meanwhile Joanne wondered if the Judge had read those headlines. The Judge claimed he always read The Sun to see what everyday people thought. Hopefully someone will have left the paper around for him to see.

Joanne thought about all the people that had helped them, they were the real heroes: Alex's headmistress who gave Alex two years at school free of charge; Sam's headmaster who and was a great friend to Sam and gave him free extra lessons through that difficult time; the QC who stuck his neck out and risked being most unpopular with the Judge; the solicitors who gave their advice, often not charging their full rates.

It was such a relief that it was all over, but it was difficult to take it all in. They had lived under such pressure and for so many years; why had the case been allowed to drag on so?

Chapter Two

The Start

Joanne could not recall exactly how she had got herself into this mess; maybe she had just been naive and impressionable, young and gullible. When she first met Gregory Franks, he seemed so clever, so important with his barrister's wig over his dark hair. He looked so grand as he strutted about the courtroom and addressed the jury. He wore pinstriped suits and conservative ties and would swagger down the corridors of the Courthouse, his black gown flowing out behind him.

Gregory had been proud of his new acquisition but, as soon as the wedding was over, everything changed. The first sign was on the first day of the honeymoon. Gregory had asked Joanne to go to the reception desk of the hotel where they were staying and get the menu to see what was for dinner that night. She had returned to the hotel room, the menu in her hand, but as she opened the door she heard Gregory on the telephone,

"Yes, that'll do. Anything really. I'm bored here. I'll be in chambers tomorrow. Bye."

Joanne handed Gregory the menu. He didn't even look at her as he said,

"Got to do a case, so we go back tonight!"

"But we've only been here one night! I thought you said no one knew where we were?"

Gregory didn't answer. That was to be his way of dealing with Joanne. He *asked* questions. He didn't *answer* questions.

"Go and pay the bill, we need to settle it now and get off!"

Joanne looked at him, puzzled. Gregory then shouted at her,

"You're the one with the money. Go and pay the bill!" he demanded.

That was the way life was to be. If they went out to a restaurant, Gregory always seemed to forget his wallet, or walk out without paying, leaving Joanne to settle the bill. Joanne bought the house in the country and put up half the money for the house in town where they lived during the week.

Gregory became more and more critical of everything Joanne did. It soon became apparent that Gregory resented Joanne's background; her large family home set in its own grounds with plenty of room for Joanne and her brothers and sisters to play; and her private education particularly irked him. Gregory was an only child. He had been brought up in a small semi-detached house on the edge of town, where kids played in the street because the back yards, some of which had been made into small gardens, were too small to play ball games. He had been sent to the local state school where he had made good progress, but there was a bitterness inside him that from time to time would ooze out. Joanne felt a bit in awe of him, he was so much older, worldly and sophisticated, a criminal law barrister and had perfected the art of dishing out scathing remarks.

Joanne was a private person. She didn't like confiding in friends. That would be letting the side down. Joanne had been brought up to believe that divorce was something that you didn't do; it was frowned upon and it was her duty to try to make the marriage work. So she decided to try the marriage guidance centre, desperate for an answer to the mess she found herself in.

Gregory complained that Joanne was not pregnant, accusing her of being infertile and useless, so Joanne also sought advice from the local fertility clinic.

That had led to five failed IVF attempts. Gregory blamed Joanne for the failures and refused to believe the possibility that he had no viable sperm.

Then out of the blue Joanne found herself pregnant. She couldn't help but feel suspicious that the clinicians had felt sorry for her and had donated the necessary sperm. But no matter, at least she was pregnant and maybe the harassment from Gregory would stop.

Sam had come into the world with blond hair and blue eyes, looking nothing like Gregory who was dark with dark brown eyes, but Joanne was fair so it did not seem too odd at the time. For a short time Gregory showed a change of attitude, now that he had a son to boast about, but it only lasted a few months before he was back to his old ways.

Then one evening Rosalind 'phoned Joanne. Rosalind was an old school friend and occasionally she called to keep in touch. Rosalind had been the subject of local village gossip; she was the village doctor's daughter and had been accused of having made it good, by entrapping the local solicitor's son!

"Come on Joanne, we need some catch-up time!" Rosalind had said on the 'phone. "How about meeting in the Thyme Café in the village, I haven't seen you for ages!"

"How will I recognise you? What will you be wearing?"

"Oh, brown skirt, brown jumper, that sort of thing!"

Great, thought Joanne, how distinctive is that? A Brown haired lady, wearing brown! Rosalind obviously hadn't changed much.

"Well in case I miss you," said Joanne cheekily, "I'll be wearing a bright pink jacket so you won't miss me!"

Rosalind was the sensible kind, she never wore make-up, she wore flat shoes, brown of course and sure enough when Joanne spotted her in the café she was wearing a brown pleated skirt and a brown V-necked jumper over a fawn blouse. This was *so* Rosalind, sensible plain colours.

Rosalind and Joanne sat opposite each other looking over the top of their coffee mugs. Rosalind hadn't changed. She still kept her hair neck-length. It was thick and brown, almost black and she had lovely hazel eyes. After exchanging how nice it was to see each other Rosalind asked Joanne what she was doing these days and how she was getting on with Gregory.

"Funny you should ask that!" said Joanne. "Things are not that good with Gregory; he's giving me such a hard time. You know something? He never even calls me by my name!"

Rosalind looked at Joanne over the top of her steaming coffee and shook her head pitifully.

"You mean you didn't notice that before?" asked Rosalind incredulously; "he *never did* call you by your name Joanne, at least not in front of me! I did say to you when he asked you to marry him, did you know what you were doing? Has he ever said he loves you?"

"No!" reflected Joanne, "That was something else. He said that he didn't need to say things like that; that it should be enough that he wanted to marry me!"

"Oh Joanne, you are so naïve! I bet he hasn't changed, I bet he still doesn't buy you flowers, or any jewellery! Don't you remember when you invited Tim and me to dinner and you showed me round the house, I asked you what things had *you* done to the house? All you could say to me was what Gregory had wanted or ordered. It wasn't your house; nothing in the house showed your touch. He shouted orders at you and you obeyed. You've been treated like this for so long you don't even notice it! But others see it. I remembered him shouting to you, "When's dinner ready?" and "Answer the 'phone will you!" I've never heard him say "Please" or "Thank you." I don't know how you put up with it! It's almost as though he enjoys hurting you; like a *nasty* little boy who's caught a butterfly in a jam jar and he has fun prodding it with sticks."

Joanne considered what Rosalind had said. She was right. It was definitely a power thing with Gregory; he had to be in control. A lump came into Joanne's throat.

It seemed to Joanne that having tried the advice of the marriage bureau and produced a son, that she really had done her duty and now had come the time to get out. Gregory was obviously never going to change.

"Well! I've done all that is humanly possible and things have just gone from bad to worse." Joanne considered the situation, "You know you don't notice it initially. It creeps up on you. Then bit-by-bit it gets worse. But you get used to it, like it doesn't really matter any more."

Joanne stared into her coffee and contemplated how it had felt and for such a long time.

"He treats me like a cigarette," she said, "he flicks it to the ground, then stamps on it. But," said Joanne looking up at Rosalind, "Gregory doesn't stop there though; he likes to rub it into the ground until only the dying embers remain."

Joanne dipped her teaspoon into her coffee and stirred the liquid round and round. She studied the small whirlpool.

"But," she said thoughtfully, "what comes around, goes around! The phoenix is part of my birth sign; and now it's my turn to turn the tables," she said with new fervour, "I will *not* be beaten. I *will* rise out of it all."

Chapter Three

Making The Break!

When Joanne told Gregory that she wanted a divorce, she was not prepared for his reaction. She wasn't quite sure what she had expected, but it was not the torrent of abuse that came flooding out.

"*Nobody* divorces me! Who the *hell* do you think you are?"

He didn't ask what he had done wrong, or what had made her want a divorce, or offer to change. He didn't even try to persuade her to stay; he just said it was her duty to stay!

Gregory dragged out the divorce proceedings for over a year; he pretended papers had not been served on him, or he just did not turn up at Court, so that a further date had to be set. Eventually in September the divorce came through and Gregory moved the last of his belongings from the house in town. Joanne was to live in the town house to which she had contributed half the money to buy and Gregory had their large Georgian mansion in the country, set in five acres of gardens. Joanne had bought the country house; after all, Gregory had reasoned at the time, she was the one with the money! Then he had insisted that she put his name on the deeds as a shared owner. What Joanne did not realise until the divorce settlement, was that Gregory had been slowly siphoning off the value of his half of the property, by taking out large loans against his share and there were huge unpaid overdrafts that had to be cleared. In the end Joanne had been forced to give Gregory the country house as part of the divorce settlement and Gregory rented a town house during the week to be near his work. The Court ordered Gregory not to come nearer than half a mile from Joanne's home, in order to protect Joanne from further harassment.

Joanne thought that was the end of the matter. She had not anticipated the onslaught that followed.

There were several incidents, but there were three that particularly stood out in her mind.

The first was on an October Monday morning and as usual, Jane, not so much a nanny, more of a sensible baby sitter, arrived early to take Sam off to the toddler group, while Joanne finished putting on her make-up and gathered her things together to go to work. Her office was only across the road, so a quick sprint usually got her there on time.

Despite the Court order to stay away from the house, Gregory still kept keys for the house and he had called round earlier that morning to look for a reference book he thought he had left there. As Joanne picked up her bag from the hall table, she noticed Gregory had left his keys partly concealed under some letters.

Gregory *never* left his keys; he was *fanatical* about having his keys with him.

Joanne picked them up; she didn't want Gregory to come back to the house with the excuse that he had left his keys behind.

She rushed to the front door and stood outside the house to see if she could see his car. Gregory had left a while ago, so maybe this was a waste of time and he had already driven off to work. Then Joanne saw Gregory's car slowly coming up the road. It was as though he had been waiting to see Joanne leave the house. Gregory proceeded to drive past her. Perplexed, Joanne ran out into the road waving the keys at him. Gregory stopped the car and furiously reversed the car back to her, wound down the car window and shouted:

"What the *hell* do you think you're doing . . . what do you want?"

"You left your keys!"

"I don't *want* the damned keys," he snapped and sped off down the road.

Bemused, Joanne walked back into the house.

As she passed through the hallway she caught sight of herself in the hall mirror and thought that her hair did not look smart enough for work. She decided to go upstairs and get some styling spray and the hair drier. She climbed the stairs and made her way down the corridor towards the bedroom, as she approached the bedroom door she thought that she could smell gas.

Puzzled, she cautiously pushed the door open. A surge of gas greeted her; it was overwhelming. What was going on? It wasn't cold enough to put on a gas fire! Joanne rushed to the bedroom windows and opened them, her heart pounding, then hurried to the gas fire and turned it to "*off*". Why was the gas on "*full*"?

Shaking, Joanne looked at her watch; she was going to be late for work. She decided to leave the windows open, after all the windows were too high up for anyone to try to break-in without a ladder and her hair would just have to do.

She ran out of the house, quickly locking the front door behind her and made her way across the road to the office.

Joanne had been fortunate to find a place of work in research so conveniently near, but she did tend to leave at the last minute. The building was a large purpose built concrete block of offices with a modern glass door entrance. There was a basic lift with a metal door which went to the 5 floors, but Joanne preferred the wide winding blue staircase with black rubber safety strips and a handy iron handrail to assist her in the run up the stairs. When she reached the second floor she went through the swing doors and down the corridor with the names of each office on the doors until she arrived at the fourth door labelled 'Research'.

As Joanne entered the office it broke the quiet atmosphere of her colleagues concentrating on their work. There were five of them, one called Barry turned round to comment,

"You're a bit late! What happened to you?" asked Barry.

Joanne sat down at her computer and tried to take her mind off things by fumbling through the post. Barry came up to her. He was a pleasant guy and was always kind, a completely laid-back guy. He was tall and straggly, probably too thin for his height and his clothes hung limply on him. His light brown hair was nearly to his shoulders and it was thinning. Joanne always thought he looked a bit like an absent-minded professor.

"What's up?" he ventured to enquire again. "You don't look very well."

Joanne wondered if she should tell him. Maybe Barry would think her completely mad, or over reacting, or imagining things.

Barry looked at Joanne's face, she was not responding in her usual bubbly way and he decided he would not pry. Sometimes, when women went all silent, he thought it best to keep clear. However, he was concerned: he had never known Joanne to be aloof.

At lunch break Barry decided he should try and find out what the problem was and invited Joanne to join him at the office canteen for a snack. Joanne accepted, she felt lonely and cold inside. Barry was relieved that she was not going to distance herself from him. He had a comfortable family life, but he sensed that Joanne was not happy. He knew that she had got her divorce and that was what she wanted. Perhaps Gregory was still causing her problems. She seemed to spend all her time at the office, although it was clear that her son Sam meant the world to her.

They sat down together with a coffee.

"Come on Joanne, what's eating you?"

Once Joanne started to tell Barry what had happened, the words came tumbling out. It felt like she was in another world. She hadn't opened up to Barry this way before, preferring to keep her private life to herself, but she needed to tell someone. Gregory just would not go away, he always found an excuse to come back to the house. It was as if he was haunting her. Punishing her. Not letting her get on with her life.

Not accepting the fact that she was free of him. Barry looked at her anxiously.

"You have to go to the police," he urged.

"You're joking! What can they do?"

"Well, I think it's all rather suspect and I'm concerned as to what's going on in Gregory's mind. Look at it logically, Joanne. It seems to me that Gregory left the house without his keys *on purpose*. Well now, he knows that you are the next one to enter the house after work at about four thirty. Jane usually brings Sam back to you some time later like about five, which gives you time, as you say, to turn yourself around before you do the cooking and bath-time thing. Isn't that what happens? Well, at four thirty it's dark. What's the first thing you would have done after opening the front door? Switch the lights on of course! By four thirty the house would have been full of gas. The whole place would have exploded. It's *obvious* Joanne, you have to report it!"

Barry went on to tell Joanne of friend of his who was advised to report harassment to the police and they had put her 'phone on '*priority*' which meant that when you call the police, they don't waste time asking a million questions. They just get there!

It all seemed too absurd to Joanne, but Barry was unusually insistent and walked with Joanne up the road to the local police station.

After a few minutes wait at the police reception area and a brief explanation as to why Joanne was there, a young policewoman invited Joanne to follow her into an interview room to make a report. She was very reassuring and told Joanne she was doing the right thing. Barry said he'd see her back at the office and having seen Joanne safely into the interview room and the door closed behind her, he left.

When Joanne walked back to work, she felt as if a load had been taken from her shoulders. Everyone was being very supportive.

At the end of the working day, when Joanne got back to the house, the smell of gas had pretty much gone. She went upstairs and shut the windows in the bedroom and stared at the old gas fire, still safely at "*off*".

The 'phone rang interrupting her thoughts. On picking up the receiver, Joanne recognised Fiona's voice,

"Oh Fiona! Thank you so much for all the tidying up and cleaning you did for me last week. The place looked great, thank you; and I'm so sorry, I *completely* forgot to leave the money out for you! I've been so preoccupied!"

"Don't you worry m'dear! I know you have a lot on your mind at the moment and, I wouldn't normally mention it, but I'm hoping to go and see m' brother in Ireland in the next week or two and I'm saving m'pennies . . ."

Fiona was a sweetie! Typically Irish. Slim and jolly. Her white hair was always perfectly permed; she dressed smartly in skirts with a jacket to match and always a silk-looking scarf about her neck.

Fiona must have been sixty-five or so. Joanne had met Fiona through Fiona's brother, David, who worked as a keeper in the local park. He had picked up a jumper a child had dropped near to the bench where Joanne sat watching Sam play with his toy truck and had asked her if the jumper belonged to them. Then David had remarked that Joanne looked tired. He had often seen her at the weekends with Sam, she was always on her own; no partner ever seemed to accompany her. David and Joanne had got into conversation and he explained that his sister Fiona worked at the Bury Hotel as head of house keeping and she wanted to retire. Fiona's eyesight was not so good these days and she found the book keeping side of things more difficult. David had offered to ask Fiona if she would like to help Joanne with the occasional cleaning of the house. That way, he reasoned, Fiona would have a bit of pocket money and Joanne would have more time to be with Sam.

So it came about that Fiona would pop round once a week and do whatever she felt needed attending to.

Fiona had really hoped to look after Sam. She loved children. She had four sons of her own. All grown up now, but one still lived with her and she had three brothers who always came round to enjoy a good Sunday lunch with her.

Joanne was aware of Fiona's hints that she would like to look after Sam, but one thing concerned Joanne and that was that Fiona occasionally had cold sores. Joanne was not medically trained, but something made her feel uneasy about the cold sores and she felt that the person who looked after Sam while she was at work had to be in excellent health. On top of that, Joanne wasn't sure if Fiona was perhaps a little too old to be looking after a toddler. So that was why Joanne had chosen Jane who was in her forties and, although

Jane had no children of her own, she had been child minding for fifteen years.

"I'm so sorry Fiona. I'll leave the money in an envelope on the hall table for you. Thank you so much for all your help."

"Not at all m' dear. So I'll not be here for a week or two. Then I'll give ye a call when I get back."

"Have a good trip Fiona!"

Joanne went downstairs and prepared Sam's tea. He would soon be back with Jane. Suddenly Joanne felt she so wanted to hug her little boy and feel him safe with her, although she knew he would be back very shortly, every minute seemed like an age.

At last Joanne could hear Jane's voice as she chatted to Sam in the hallway. Jane always chatted cheerfully away, even though Sam was too young to understand everything she said. Joanne sighed with relief. So at least *some* things were normal! She rushed into the hall and bent down to pick Sam out of the buggy. She hugged him close to her and looked up gratefully at Jane,

"Let's all have a hot cup of tea together."

After Jane had gone home and Sam had eaten his tea, Joanne played a while with Sam, then gave him his bath and put him safely in his cot bed that had sides to stop him falling out. Sam curled up with his teddy under his arm and his thumb in his mouth while Joanne sat on the floor next to him watching him until he fell asleep. Everything seemed quite normal, but Joanne's stomach still felt in knots. It was a comforting thought that Sam always slept in her room; she needed to keep him safe with her. She loved to watch Sam as he slept; he always looked so angelic, his blond hair falling over the pillow. He was a pretty child and he meant the world to Joanne.

Going back downstairs Joanne wondered about watching TV, but she still felt uneasy.

Suddenly there was a loud banging on the front door. Joanne just sat there. Who was it at this time of night? She looked at her watch. Why should she answer the door?

The banging started again and now there was a loud voice shouting. Joanne went out into the hall.

"Open the bloody door! Open the bloody door!" It was Gregory. It sounded as though he was completely crazy, maybe even drunk.

"I need to get some things!" he bellowed.

Joanne knew there was no point in reminding Gregory that the Court had ordered him not approach the house; better to let him in, she thought and let him get whatever he wanted, rather than have an argument, she knew he could be very violent. Joanne went to open the door. When Gregory came into the light of the hallway, Joanne barely recognised him. He had a grey pallor and eyes looked glazed and bloodshot.

Maybe he had expected everything to be gone; the house blown up; all his problems solved in one blast? Maybe he had been dwelling on the cruelty of it all, but oh what a plan and would he get away with it? Would everyone believe his story; that he had left his keys in the house, that Joanne was the only one with keys and that in her desperate state of mind she had decided to blow herself up with the house?

What had he come back for?

Gregory picked up his keys from the hall table then left the house. Joanne wondered what had been going through his mind all day. It seemed to Joanne, looking at Gregory's distraught and puffy face, that things had not quite gone as he had expected. Had Gregory been preparing this look? Was he trying to appear to be mourning his loss? That was probably the face he planned to show to the world.

The next incident was about two weeks later. The day started just like any other day. Jane arrived to pick up Sam and take him to his toddler group. After polite exchanges about how the weekend had gone, Jane strapped Sam in his pushchair and waved goodbye to Joanne who blew goodbye kisses until they disappeared from view.

Joanne then made her way to work. She swung into the office and threw her bag on the floor next to her desk and eagerly opened the post to see what was today's challenge! Sometimes she was given the task of pulling out some interesting data; well, she could always hope!

Barry had his head down in some figures as usual. Mary was on the 'phone with another consultant discussing a new patient that had been admitted. Mary was not far off from retirement, but she kept herself trim and dressed in smart, soft coloured, feminine suits, with her grey hair swept back in a short modern style. She loved her work as a paediatrician and worked with a passion, doing research in childhood diseases.

After a while Joanne felt a stabbing pain in her stomach. It wasn't the time for her period and anyway it was not in the right place, it felt higher up.

"Aaah!" Joanne moaned, bending over and hugging her stomach.

"What's up?" asked Barry in a half listening way, he didn't look up, he was far too engrossed in his figures.

"It feels like pieces of glass sticking into my stomach," groaned Joanne. Barry didn't seem to hear her, his attention was miles away.

Joanne concentrated on trying to cope with the pain, wracking her brain as to what it could be.

Mary finished her conversation on the 'phone and turned round to speak to Joanne. Joanne slowly rocked herself to and fro in an effort to contain the pain.

Mary couldn't quite make Joanne out. Joanne was bright and yet she had taken this post that she could do standing on her head, managing to get through an enormous amount of work in very little time. In fact Mary had highlighted this in Joanne's end of contract report, saying that she was a valuable member of the team and recommending that Joanne's contract should be renewed. Maybe Joanne needed the short flexible hours, she had a child and short hours did not go hand in hand with more demanding positions.

Looking at Joanne now, it seemed all out of character. Mary shouted to get Barry's attention,

"Barry!" she shouted to get his attention, "I think you should take Joanne across the road to Dr Leonard's surgery."

Barry looked up, obviously his mind elsewhere. Mary glared at him, this guy was just *so* laid back. However, she needed someone laid back to deal with crashing computers, someone who didn't mind spending hours pondering over problems and fixing them. She smiled to herself as she thought that sometimes Barry seemed so laid back that he was in danger of falling over! Mary decided that she needed to take the situation in hand. She repeated, firmly:

"Barry!" "Now!"

As Barry and Joanne entered Dr Leonard's reception room, the secretary glanced up. You could almost read her face; one more patient meant not getting out to lunch on time.

"Fill out this form will you?" she said in a bored, robotic fashion, handing a form and a pen to Barry.

Joanne sat doubled-up on the chair, the pain just would not go away, it felt like it was grinding a hole inside her. Barry sat next to her with his arm round her back trying to comfort her.

After a while a doctor came into the room and handed the receptionist a note. Looking over the patients in the room, he motioned to Barry.

"What do we have here? You'd better bring her through!"

The doctor wasn't sure what it was, but he wasn't taking any chances. He scribbled a note, faxed it across to the local A&E department and then handed the original to Barry.

"Just get her in a taxi and take her straight round to casualty," he instructed.

φ

When Joanne woke up she found herself lying in a hospital bed with faded curtains drawn around it for privacy. She could hear doctors and nurses talking and moving outside the curtains, attending to other patients. She looked to see if she could read her watch, no watch! Her handbag? No handbag! Then a doctor put his head through the curtains.

"How are you feeling? Any more pain?"

Joanne shook her head and tried to sit up.

"It feels a lot better. Tender, but no real pain. What time is it?"

"Four o'clock. Don't worry, one of the nurses has put your belongings away for safety. I'll get someone to get them for you."

Joanne relaxed back onto the pillow.

"Crumbs . . ." she said, "I've been here all day. I have to get back for my son."

"Well, you could go home now. The gentleman who brought you in left his number, he said you should call him and he would come and fetch you," and he handed Barry's card with his mobile number to Joanne.

Joanne wasn't going to trouble Barry; she had to look after herself. Barry had his own family to care for.

Joanne made her way home in a taxi. During the journey she tried to make sense of the day. She felt dazed, confused. She hadn't even asked the doctor what he thought could have caused the pain? She must have slept for hours, what had happened during that time? She tried to go through the events of the day. What had she eaten for breakfast? Just the normal cereal?

Joanne always made her own mixture from various fruits and oats then left them to soak in milk. But, hadn't she been upstairs drying her hair when she had heard Gregory let himself into the house to collect something from the dining room cupboard?

Once home, Joanne quickly thumbed through Yellow Pages for the local locksmith. She had to change the lock, that was the only way to feel safe.

Chapter Four

A Chance Meeting

It was Friday, a dark January evening, after a long day at work. Joanne went to the ladies room to freshen up her makeup. Everybody seemed to have gone home. It was so quiet. She took her time applying a bit more mascara, which she had not been put on too well first thing that morning.

Suddenly there was a huge clatter against the door and Mary came bursting in, banging the books in her arms against the door. She made such a noise it made Joanne jump.

Distracted, Joanne let the mascara brush slip and it caught her eye.

"Damn!" she groaned quietly to herself and her eye started to sting.

"Sorry to startle you!" bustled Mary, "Are you okay?"

"Yes. Yes. I'm fine . . . just tired," Joanne dabbed her tearing eye. "It'll stop streaming in a moment. I've just got such sensitive eyes!"

As Joanne walked home the pain seemed to get worse. Every time Joanne blinked, she felt a sharp stabbing pain and her eye was watering so much she couldn't see.

Once in the hallway of her house, she felt around for the 'phone. The pain was excruciating. She put her hand over her right eyelid to keep it closed and with her left eye, tried to focus on the entries in her diary for Dr. Lumb's 'phone number.

The secretary answered. She said that Dr Lumb was on holiday and his partner, Dr Chris Parry, had left an hour and a half ago to see some post-operative patients at the hospital. She said that he would probably go on home afterwards, but she would leave a message on his mobile.

Joanne was exhausted; she sat down on the hall chair, keeping her hand firmly on her eyelid to keep it closed.

After a while the 'phone rang. Joanne quickly picked it up.

"Joanne Franks? It's Chris Parry. I heard you rang my secretary, what can I do for you?"

"Oh thank you so much for calling!" said Joanne in relief and she explained what had happened.

"The problem is that my eye hurts so much I daren't open it and it keeps watering all the time!"

"Where are you?"

"I'm at home!"

"Where's home? I've finished for the day and I could come out to see you."

"Oh! That's so kind. I would be so grateful."

Joanne gave her address and sat and waited. She felt calmer now, but her eye was throbbing. She closed both her eyes, but somehow it felt better to keep her hand on her right eyelid to keep it closed.

About twenty minutes must have gone by when Joanne heard a car draw up outside. With one hand held over her eye, she stood up and went towards the front door and listened, desperately hoping it would be Dr Parry. The bell rang and Joanne opened the door with the other hand. It was such a relief to see him standing there. He looked at the troubled Joanne,

"Joanne Franks?"

"Yes! Yes! That's me!"

"Chris Parry, but please call me Chris," he introduced himself, "Please sit down Joanne and let's have a look." He peered at her right eye, "Um. Yes! It does look sore!"

He put his black briefcase on the hall table and took out various small packets of eye drops, his portable slit lamp and blue light.

"Lean back and relax, I'm going to put some anaesthetic eye drops in, to ease the pain."

Chris gently eased open her eyelid just enough to pop in the eye drop.

"Now Joanne, just keep your eyes closed and give it a moment or two. It should soon feel better."

Joanne relaxed with her eyes closed. She could feel the pain slowly receding. It was so good to feel cared for and something else, it was so nice to hear him call her by her name.

"How does it feel now?" asked Chris.

Joanne tried to open her eye,

"Much better thank you . . . but still a bit weird!"

"Well. Now let's look at the damage."

Chris picked up some different drops and popped one in her eye.

"Blink a bit," he said, "now look at me." Chris held his portable slit lamp and examined Joanne's eye.

"Well Joanne. You've got a nasty abrasion there."

Chris took out a new bottle of eye drops and opening the bottle put a couple more drops in her eye.

"This is an antibiotic," he said, "you need to put a drop in your eye every four hours and this," he said handing her a pink tube, "is a lubricant you put in at night. It will make your vision blurry, but it will act as a protective layer while you sleep. And this is a anti-inflammatory to ease the pain if necessary."

Chris packed the rest of the eye drops back into his bag, along with his portable slit lamp and light and zipped it up. Then he reached into the inside pocket of his jacket and pulled out a card and handed it to Joanne.

"Here's my card. It's got my mobile number on it. Please feel free to call me over the weekend if your eye doesn't improve. Actually Joanne, call me anyway to let me know how you're getting on."

Chris held out his hand to shake Joanne's. She could open both eyes now and she could see properly. There was something very special about this man, with his fair hair swept back from his face and his warm grey eyes; his whole presence seemed so caring. His pale grey suit made him look taller and slimmer than she had expected and he obviously liked colourful bow-ties. As he shook Joanne's hand, the feel of his skin on hers just felt so good.

By Sunday evening Joanne's eye felt much better. The eye was no longer red and although it was still a bit scratchy, the pain was under control. She wondered if she dare call Chris. When was the better time to call him? Sunday when he wasn't working, or Monday, a normal working day? Joanne opted for the Sunday, as no doubt Chris would be snowed under with patients on Monday.

Joanne dialled Chris's mobile number. It went straight to his answer 'phone.

"This is the answer-phone for Chris Parry. I'm sorry I'm not here to take your call personally, but please leave a message and I'll call you back as soon as I can."

Joanne panicked at hearing Chris's voice. She rang off quickly. He sounded so nice, but she wasn't sure what to say. If she was going to leave a message, she'd better work out what she was going to say.

Joanne took a deep breath and dialled the number again. This time she left a message.

"Hi, this is Joanne Franks. My eye is much better. Thank you so much for coming round on Friday, I'm so very grateful to you."

It was later that evening that Joanne got a call back from Chris. It was so wonderful to hear his voice again. He sounded quite formal, but at the same time warm and caring.

"Thank you for your call Joanne. Sorry I must have been out of range. I'd like to see you tomorrow if that's at all possible, just to make sure your eye is progressing the way it should. No doubt the patient list will be very booked up, but probably five thirty or six would be a good time. Do call my secretary tomorrow and ask her to fit you in."

Joanne felt nervous. She wanted to see Chris again, she liked Chris and that was what made her feel uneasy. Well anyway, she reasoned with herself, she had to have her eye checked out, so she had better arrange for Jane to look after Sam.

φ

Dr Lumb and Chris shared the same consulting rooms situated in a Victorian town house. Joanne sat in the large waiting room, anxiously waiting her turn to be seen. She felt warm after walking most of the way and unbuttoned her parka. She looked around the room at the traditional furniture and the fine art paintings on the wall, all of which made her think that the room had been decorated in an older person's taste. There was a grand piano at one end and a large round mahogany dining table in the middle of the room, with magazines arranged in orderly piles. Joanne looked at the windows on two sides of the room, a typical impersonal waiting room. Three of the windows faced the street and the other three looked as though they faced a garden. Joanne went over to the dining table to choose a magazine. Maybe she should try to read one, even if she felt too nervous to read. She chose a Vogue and after checking that it was the current month's edition, she went back to her seat. Flicking through the pages, she was pleased to see that the silk skirt and high heels that she wore were still in fashion, not that she was a fashion slave, just nice to know that they were still in vogue, so to speak!

Joanne was the last patient in the waiting room; everyone else had gone. Suddenly she was aware of someone looking at her from the doorway. It was Chris. He stood there in his formal light grey suit. Joanne could see him properly now, rather than squinting through a sore eye and his tall slim figure impressed her. He caught her eye and motioned her to follow him to his consulting room. She stood up and walked towards him. He made her feel good.

Chris opened the consulting room door and offered to take Joanne's coat. She slipped her parka off her shoulders and tried to appear calm as she handed it to him. Chris asked her to take her place in the examination chair and he sat opposite her, he told her to place her chin on the chin rest of the apparatus and let him examine her eye.

When it appeared that he had almost finished, Joanne asked conversationally,

"Did you manage to get a good break at Christmas?"

"Oh, not bad . . . in a family sort of way!"

"Oh! Do you have children as well?"

Chris laughed.

"No, no! What I meant was, that Christmas was spent visiting relatives, I stayed at my parent's place. I'm not married!"

Joanne told him that she was divorced and that she'd spent her Christmas pretty much the same way. They chatted about this and that, although all the time Joanne hardly heard the words. She just kept looking at Chris's angular face, staring into his grey eyes and listening to the sound of his comforting voice. Then it seemed the conversation was over and Chris stood up. He picked up Joanne's parka from the settee and handed it to her. Looking into his eyes, she thanked him and held out her hand to shake his and then Chris escorted Joanne to the secretary's office.

The young secretary sat at her desk in her prim white coat with her shiny red hair held back in a neat ponytail. She was fumbling inside her handbag on her knee. The desk looked clear of papers as though she had finished for the day, the only sign of work to be done was stacked tidily in two paper trays to one side, marked "In" and "Out". She looked up when Chris led Joanne to her desk and seemed surprised when Chris turned to leave the room, glancing briefly at Joanne, before disappearing down the corridor.

The secretary leant over her desk and called after him,

"You haven't left me a fee note."

"No," he called back over his shoulder, "no charge!"

The secretary's smooth face creased into a frown and she appeared disgruntled. She didn't like working late and she wasn't sure that Dr Lumb, the senior partner, would approve if Chris were not charging this patient.

Driving back home Joanne suddenly started to panic. She *couldn't* and *mustn't* become fond of this man, or even *think* of it. She had been through enough, there was no way she could risk repeating anything like that again. She drove on towards her house, but her mind kept drifting back to the consulting room. She kept seeing Chris's face, his eyes, the way his hand felt when he shook hers, the way he looked at her as he handed her parka to her. Was it possible that Chris was attracted to her? Why wasn't he charging her for coming out to see her and for her follow-up appointment today?

She parked the car outside her house and sat there for a while trying to make sense of one minute having a fluttering feeling of excitement inside her and the next minute a feeling of fear that he could just turn out to be another Gregory. But no . . . Chris was different, definitely different. There was no way he was like anyone Joanne had ever met before.

The next day Joanne couldn't help reading and re-reading Chris's business card. She put it in her wallet and closed her handbag and then she opened her handbag, took out her wallet and studied the card again. Finally she plucked up the courage to call him.

"I just wanted to say thank you so much for seeing me yesterday and sorting out my eye. If you won't let me pay you for coming out to see me, maybe you could at least let me buy you a drink. There's a really nice wine bar on Orchard Street, do you know it?"

"No, I don't, but it sounds a nice idea. Thank you. How about after work then? What time do you finish?"

"Five thirty."

"Well I could probably make it by six if that's ok? How about Wednesday? Where do I collect you?"

Joanne gave her work address, she was now so excited, but also so scared. Then another blow of panic hit her. Did Chris know she had a little son? Of course not! How could he. Had she mentioned it in the consulting room? She doubted it. Maybe he had seen the childish toys or seen the pushchair in the hallway when he called at her house? Or maybe not.

The rest of the day Joanne spent worrying about what to do. Should she call Chris now and tell him, or tell him when they met up again?

Eventually Joanne felt she just had to call him. She couldn't bare the uncertainty any longer. She just had to tell him that she had a son. Would he be shocked? Would he disapprove and not wish to see her?

It was ten thirty in the evening when Joanne finally plucked up the courage to 'phone Chris. He answered the 'phone rather sleepily,

"Joanne? Oh . . . um . . . sorry . . . I'm in bed."

"Oh I'm so sorry . . . it's just that I need to tell you something!"

"Ok! But can't it wait until tomorrow?"

"It's just that I have a little boy, he's two and a half . . ."

"Don't worry about it. I'm looking forward to seeing you tomorrow. Tomorrow at six, don't worry about it . . . I'll see you tomorrow."

Phew! Joanne felt such a relief. At least Chris knew now and it didn't seem to put him off, but she still felt a bit anxious.

At work, the day seemed to drag on and on. Joanne couldn't concentrate on her work. But at last it was five fifty and Joanne made her way to reception and waited for Chris to arrive. Sure enough, at exactly six o'clock, Chris appeared at the glass entrance doors and he looked so good . . .

It was dark as they walked up Orchard Street to the wine bar. Walking inside they were greeted by a blazing log fire, the smell of wine and the gentle murmur of people chatting cosily together.

Chris and Joanne found a table in the corner and chose a bottle of Bordeaux. They sat and enjoyed the warmth of the fire, the candles on the table and bit-by-bit they she felt a glow inside, as the wine started to make Joanne feel relaxed. She so desperately wanted to hold Chris's hand. He had been so kind to her and she so wanted to show him how much this meant to her. But Chris was a doctor and wasn't it correct that doctors were not meant to show any affection towards their patients? Maybe it had to be up to Joanne to show her feelings?

Chris's hands were on the table, one hand holding his glass of wine, but the other was free. He was talking about his practice and the pressures of work, when she took the opportunity to slip her hand in his. Chris looked at her and squeezed her hand affectionately and they sat there, just like that, for two hours chatting about this and that and all about their lives. It seemed that they had a whole lifetime to catch up on.

The bar assistant put another log on the fire and flames danced around it making a lively crackling noise. Above the fireplace Joanne noticed the clock. Oh dear! Was it really that late? The time had just gone so quickly.

"I'd better get back for Sam," said Joanne anxiously, "Jane doesn't like to stay much after nine; she lives quite a long way out of town."

Chris helped Joanne with her parka and they set off down the road, hand in hand.

Suddenly Chris stopped and pulled Joanne towards him, giving her a long slow kiss that made her melt inside . . . she'd always wanted to feel that way. It was perfect. Joanne had never felt like this before, she wanted the feeling to go on and on forever . . . it was beautiful.

Chapter Five

The Final Straw

There it was again, the heavy banging on Joanne's front door. It was six o'clock in the evening. Jane had gone home, Sam had just finished his tea and was playing on the kitchen floor while Joanne washed up.

Not again! Joanne could not believe that Gregory would just not go away. He was a barrister for goodness sake! Wasn't he meant to obey the law? Or did he feel he was above it? Gregory had been ordered by the Court to remove all his belongings and not to come near the house, but he persisted making excuses to come back. He had his own place, as well at the country house, what more could he want? Yet he continued to harass Joanne, as though he was trying to haunt her, punish her for leaving him.

Then came the shouting.

"How dare you change the locks! Damn you! Open this door! Now!"

Joanne braced herself against the kitchen sink, her heart started to pound. Sam looked up at her anxiously, wondering what was going to happen next.

Bang . . . bang . . . bang.

Would the banging and shouting never stop?

Maybe the best way to defuse things was to let Gregory in, let him get what he wanted and hope that after he had given her the usual verbal abuse, he would leave without too much damage being done.

As soon as Joanne unlocked the door, Gregory pushed it open, thrusting it against her, trapping her against the wall behind and stormed ahead into the kitchen.

Sam had taken refuge on the hall stairs, crouched into a little ball and watched nervously. He could see his mum through the kitchen doorway. He wanted to be near her, but he hoped he was safely out of the way of any crossfire.

Joanne's handbag was on the island unit in the kitchen. As Joanne entered the kitchen, Gregory grabbed her handbag, held it above his head, in a taunting fashion and then flung it across the room. The handbag hit the wall and the contents fell scattered across the floor.

"Please," begged Joanne, "what do you want . . . please . . . just get what you want and leave us alone . . ."

"Nobody locks me out . . . come here you . . ." and he grabbed Joanne's arm. She was wearing her grandmother's gold bracelet. Gregory grabbed the gold band and twisted it, turning it as hard as he could, while watching Joanne's face to see how much pain he could inflict. Then the bracelet snapped. The metal cut into Joanne's wrist and blood started to run down her arm. Joanne retreated behind the island unit and slid down onto the floor in shock, staring at the blood. She reached for a tea towel and wrapped it tightly around her wrist. She could hear Gregory as he threw things around the room in rage. The 'phone was on the island unit shelf, just in front of her. If only she could reach it without Gregory noticing.

Carefully, Joanne felt for the 'phone cord and gently pulled the 'phone towards her.

She dialled 999. Joanne could hear the operator, she started asking questions, Joanne didn't dare say anything, but she knew they could trace the call. She lay the handset quietly on its side next to the 'phone. Gregory continued to shout and hurl abuse. Then Joanne pleaded,

"Please . . . please don't hurt me anymore. Just take what you want and leave us alone . . ." she knew that would be enough to give the police operator an idea of what was going on.

It wasn't long before a police van drew up outside the house. This time the banging on the door was welcome. Gregory stopped his ranting and raving and came over to where Joanne sat huddled on the floor.

Seeing the 'phone hand set on its side, he shouted,

"What the *hell* have you done now you . . ." and made his way to the front door.

Joanne heard Gregory open the door and speak to someone. Then the voices became more raised and she could hear people coming inside the house.

Joanne heard an officer say,

"Now Sir, please be calm, we just need to satisfy ourselves that all is well . . . we've had a call from this address and it is our duty is to make sure all is well . . ."

Gregory quickly put on his charming act.

"Officer I can assure that everything is fine . . . you had a call from this address? Impossible! You must be mistaken . . . are you sure . . . ah . . . well then . . . it must be Joanne. Joanne is mad you know, completely mad, she does crazy things . . . she's fine though, completely fine . . ."

"I'm sorry Sir, but we have to see for ourselves. Who else is in the house?"

The officers were all the while making their way towards the kitchen; Joanne could hear that there must be at least four of them.

She could just see from her position on the floor that it was a policewoman who was the first to enter the kitchen, while two male officers guided Gregory towards the living room. Even in her formal uniform, the policewoman seemed kind and attentive. She bent over Joanne and helped her up. She called out to the other offices,

"She's been hurt," and she examined Joanne's wrist.

A male officer entered the kitchen and told the two of them to wait there while the other officers interviewed Gregory.

It wasn't long before Joanne heard the officers escort Gregory out to the police van. She could hear Gregory protesting,

"I can manage by myself . . ."

The policewoman told Joanne that Gregory would be taken to the local Police Station and held there. Then, looking at Joanne's arm she said,

"I think you should see a doctor, it looks as though the cut is not so bad . . . but there's a lot of bruising . . ."

A balloon of blood under the skin was working its way up Joanne's arm,

"I know a doctor I can call . . ."

"Well . . . ok . . . if you are sure you are all right . . ." said the policewoman and she left to join the other officers.

Joanne picked up the 'phone, shaking. She began to cry. Cry with relief that the incident was over. She called Chris.

Chris in his usual calm manner asked Joanne to describe the injury and assured her that she would be ok; it just looked awful and would be painful. He would call her after he got home from the hospital.

Joanne went upstairs to find little Sam. He was in his usual place, hiding in her bed, the covers pulled over his head. Sam had the child-like wisdom to hide and get himself out of the way when he was frightened. Joanne sat down on the floor next to the bed, so that she was on the same level as Sam's head. She gently pulled the covers back a little way and kissed his cheek.

"It's all over now . . . come and have a cuddle."

At eight in the evening Chris called Joanne,

"I really think that you and Sam should not stay in that house any longer. Gregory will never leave you alone . . . its not safe for you to remain there. I'll come and collect you at about eight thirty. It's starting to rain so wrap up warmly . . ."

φ

Joanne and Sam stood together on the pavement, in the dark. The rain began to get heavier and Joanne snuggled Sam inside her parka, the quilted lining and fur hood keeping them warm and dry. The streetlights weren't very bright, but it was enough to see the outline of the road through the rain.

Then Joanne saw the bright headlamp of a motorbike approaching and hearing the powerful roar of the engine she hoped that this was Chris. Yes it was. She was so thankful and reassured to see him as he drew up next to them.

Once on the motorbike, Joanne could relax. Chris had fitted a comfortable pillion seat for his passengers, so that there was no difficulty in positioning little Sam between them. That was typical of Chris, he was always thoughtful of other people rather than himself. Joanne could not believe how lucky she was to have met this incredible man. She put her arms round Chris's waist to hold on and to cradle little Sam between them. Joanne's legs were just touching Chris's. She could feel the warmth of his body through his trousers; it felt delicious, keeping her warm as they sped off home.

Home . . . yes . . . and that's what it was from then on.

Chapter Six

A New Beginning

Chris had bought his house, with his parent's help, when he was a student and had lived there ever since. It was a pretty white-bricked house with a red tiled roof, set back from the road with a wide paved driveway. As they approached the house a lamp came on under a small porch above the wooden front door and a welcoming light shone from inside the house through vertical glass panels running down the length of the door. Joanne thought that outside looked a bit bare and the unswept leaves on the paving stones looked soggy in the pouring rain. It needed some colour, she thought, maybe some plants and pretty creepers to climb the white walls.

The ground floor of the house was open plan, light coloured oak floorboards stretched throughout. The kitchen at one end with light wood fittings, a modern mahogany dining table and chairs in the middle of the room set on a rug of warm yellows and oranges. At the far end of the room, a cream settee was placed before French windows and a glass-topped table was strewn with books and magazines. Joanne liked the layout; she could imagine herself watching little Sam play while she was busy in the kitchen area.

Joanne pulled some junior Lego and a small teddy from her large parka pockets and gave them to Sam. She wasn't a fan of big pockets, but this time they had been useful; then she hung up her parka to dry on some hooks next to the front door. Sam settled himself down on the rug next to the French windows overlooking the garden, absorbed in his toys.

Chris was standing in the kitchen area making some mugs of hot tea. Joanne joined him. It all seemed so tranquil here. Sam no longer felt it necessary to run up to her, pull at her clothes and try to drag her across the room to be next to him. He played contentedly with his Lego. Maybe Sam could sense the feeling of peace and security. Joanne felt Chris's arms around her and she closed her eyes enjoying the feeling of warmth and love and felt blissfully happy.

Later that evening, Joanne carried a sleepy Sam upstairs to what was to become his bedroom. Chris had already made up a bed in the corner of the room with a light blue duvet and pillows and he had scattered several colourful cushions on the bed for decoration. A small bedside lamp was on the floor near to the bed-head and at the foot of the bed Chris had placed a packet of 'night pants'.

Chris watched Joanne and Sam anxiously from the bedroom doorway, hoping they would feel at home.

"I didn't know exactly what to get, but I found those at the local chemist and thought you might need them for Sam."

"They're fine! Perfect! Thank you so much, you have thought of everything!"

Joanne placed cushions round the edge of Sam's bed so that he would not fall out, or at least he would have a soft landing. She pulled off her shirt and slipped it under the duvet so that it covered him. That way she knew that when he woke up he would not panic and worry where he was. Joanne knew that if Sam could smell the scent of her from her shirt, he would realise that she was not far away. She brushed aside his blond hair, kissed his sleepy forehead and tucked his small brown teddy next to him. Then she sat on the floor by the bed to watch him a while and make sure that he was properly asleep.

Feeling content that Sam was settled for the night, Joanne got up from the floor and quietly slipped out of the room. She left the bedroom door slightly ajar so that the landing light would shine into Sam's room, she didn't want Sam to wake up and find himself in the dark and not know where he was.

Joanne walked quietly across the corridor. Opposite was Chris's study and through the partly open door she could see the flickering lights of the computer and bookshelves, over-stuffed with books and his desk covered in papers.

Creeping upstairs to the second floor she saw the bathroom ahead of her and to the right of that, was Chris's bedroom. A soft light shone through his half open bedroom door and she could just hear some music playing gently in the background.

Joanne slowly pushed the door further open and saw Chris lying in the bed, he was reading a computer magazine and waiting for her. As she approached he pulled the duvet back and got out of bed to greet her and in the peace and tranquillity of the room they explored each other . . . all night.

φ

Everything felt so right. It all seemed so natural, Chris's parents, Anne Marie and Douglas, warmly welcomed Joanne and made her feel as though she had always belonged in the family. Joanne's parents got on well with Anne Marie and Douglas, they found they had similar interests and hobbies, which made for easy conversation and soon wedding plans were underway.

June 5th was a brilliantly hot sunny day. A small country wedding in the local church, with a sympathetic vicar, followed by the reception in a marquee in the garden at Joanne's parents place. It was the most wonderful day. Joanne and Chris stayed at a romantic old manor house for a few nights, while Joanne's parents looked after Sam. Chris was the most wonderful lover. Joanne had never known such tenderness and the heights of pleasure he took her to were more than she ever dreamed possible.

Back home Joanne filled plant pots with flowers and planted creepers to grow up the walls of the house and cascade around the front door. Sam played happily with the other children in the road, he had settled in well at the local school and life at last life seemed to Joanne to be just as it should be, a normal family life with love, happiness and tenderness, everything she had never had before.

Putting Sam to bed at night always made her feel so grateful. At last she had a loving and secure home for her little boy and Chris was the most amazingly attentive father. Joanne loved to watch Sam as he slept; he looked so angelic with his arms wrapped around his teddy; and now another warmth and excitement swept through her body as she felt the new baby move inside her.

The arrival of Alex was such a happy time for Chris and Joanne, he was everything a couple could hope for, he was a beautiful baby with blond hair and blue eyes, he was healthy and suckled well at Joanne's breasts. The interrupted nights were worth it! Alex was a bright and cheerful and made the family complete.

Sam loved making Lego models for Alex and brought them to him to admire, he longed for Alex to play rough and tumble with him and asked Joanne,

"When will Alex be able to play footy with me mum?"

But, while waiting for Alex's football skills to develop, they played many other games. Every cardboard box that came into the house was made into a vehicle for Alex and Sam pushed him at great speed on the polished wooden floor. They made pancakes with Chris and both boys loved mixing and tossing them, sometimes successfully, followed by a lot of icing sugar that seemed to go everywhere! Bath times were extravagant bubble emporiums with bubbles of all colours reaching up to the boys' necks and toys were spread throughout the house. When it came to kissing the boys goodnight, Chris and Joanne would often find that they had made a den out of the beds with cardboard boxes, pillows and duvet covers and inside they would find two little boys asleep surrounded by their teddies.

Chapter Seven

Payback Time

The morning post fell with a thud on the doormat. Joanne bent down and started to sort through the letters, bills and circulars. Then she felt her stomach tighten into a knot. She stared again at the brown envelope in her hand with the Courts stamp on it. What could it contain? She cautiously eased the envelope open and pulled out the white sheet and opened it out. It had the Courts coat of arms on the left hand side and the letter was headed,

"In the Principal Registry of the Family Division," and underneath was the word,

"Order." Then there was Sam's name and it stated,

"To: Joanne Parry (Formerly Franks). If you do not obey the paragraph (2) of this order you will be guilty of contempt of court and you may be sent to prison."

Wow! That's a bit tough, thought Joanne. They certainly like to be heavy handed. She continued to read down,

"Upon hearing The Father, Gregory Franks on a without notice application and upon reading the statement of the Father it is ordered (1). That this case be listed for consideration of Contact between The Father, Gregory Franks before the Honourable Mr Justice Black on Monday March 8, 1993. (2). The Mother Joanne Parry (Formerly Franks) must personally attend at the said hearing."

A cold fear gripped Joanne's heart. Why, after all this time was Gregory applying to the Court to have access to Sam?

Joanne sat down on the hall stairs and buried her head in her hands. It felt like a blow to her stomach. Tears started to well up in her eyes and she felt the old panic come flooding back, the awful feeling of helplessness, like a trapped animal. *How could he do this?* How could he stir up everything again? Sam was a happy five year old, settled in the local school and popular with his school friends. How could she explain to Sam, that the man that he had watched hit his mum and shout abuses, now demanded access to him? What kind of sense did that make? Why unsettle a child and to what purpose? To please an adult, or to get back at Joanne or was it just to mess up their lives?

Joanne tried to work out what was going on in Gregory's mind. Gregory had never shown an interest in Sam. He'd never fed him; never picked him up; never pushed him in his pushchair; and never played with him. If Joanne had wanted to go out and Gregory was in the house; Gregory would not look after Sam, Joanne had to organise a babysitter!

She remembered the only time she had left Sam in a room with Gregory had been when Sam was two years old and they were staying at the country house. Some of Gregory's friends had called round and Gregory had told Joanne to go and prepare some tea and biscuits for them. Sam was in the sitting room playing on the floor and Joanne had asked Gregory to keep an eye on Sam.

"Of course!" Gregory had snapped. He did not even look up at her, but continued his conversation with his friends.

When Joanne reappeared in the sitting room carrying the tray of tea and biscuits, Sam was nowhere to be seen.

"Where's Sam?" asked Joanne as she placed the tray on a table in the middle of the room and looked around for him. Gregory had looked up at her, shrugged his shoulders and carried on talking. Joanne walked around the room looking behind the chairs in case Sam was hiding, playing with a car or something. But Sam was nowhere to be seen. Where could he be? He couldn't have gone far. Joanne quickly walked out of the sitting room, closed the door behind her and started to call his name,

"Sam! Sam! Where are you? Please come to mummy Sam. Sam where are you?"

There was no response. Joanne told herself to be calm and methodical; she must look carefully in each room in turn. He was only two years old he couldn't have gone far. Then she ran upstairs and carefully looked into each room calling out his name. Still no Sam. Back downstairs, Joanne made her way into the shadowy entrance hall and she saw a streak of light coming from the front door. It wasn't properly closed! She grabbed her jacket from the hall cloak peg and pulled the door open. Surely Sam would not wander outside on his own? Joanne ran around the outside the house, calling his name and then she made her way into the garden. This is crazy, she said to herself. How long had she been making the tea? Twenty minutes maybe?

How far could Sam wander in that time and where to? Joanne continued down the neatly mown lawn. It was an informal garden, mostly lawn with borders of decorative shrubs, cherry and crab apple trees. At the end of the garden the grass had been allowed to grow naturally tall as it went down to a shallow stream, where clear water ambled over small pebbles. This was far too far for Sam to have wandered and Joanne turned round and started to walk back up the garden. Then she thought she heard a snivelling sound. She stopped, turned round and went back to the edge of the stream and looked carefully along the narrow bank. Then she saw something move. It was Sam! He was higher up the stream trying to crawl up the muddy bank. His hair was wet, water dripping down his face and the front of the T-shirt and trousers were soaked. The pebbles could be very slippery with moss. He must have slipped face down into the water. Joanne rushed to the bank edge and pulled him up into her arms.

"Oh Sam! Sam! What were you doing? You mustn't leave the house without mummy! Oh you're so cold and wet!" and she held him against her to warm him up, pulling her jacket around him. Sam put his arms around her neck and snuggled his face into her hair as she carried him back up the garden to the house. What had he been doing? Maybe he had been throwing twigs into the water to watch them make their way down stream, she didn't know, but she signed a sign of relief that he was safe. Then a shiver went through her at the thought that he could have knocked his head and drowned. People say you can drown in only a few inches of water. As Joanne carried Sam through the front door she remembered thinking how strange it was that no one had come out of the sitting room to ask if they were all right, or to ask if Sam had been found. They must have heard Joanne calling out while looking for Sam, but no, nobody had been interested.

Gregory had never paid any attention to Sam before, so why the interest now?

Chapter Eight

Rewind to 1993

Vengeance?

So the Courts, in their wisdom, demanded that Sam visit Gregory every Saturday for three weeks, for Sam to get used to visiting him. Then the visits were to be increased to include Saturday to Sunday evening, on alternate weekends.

This was the first of the eighty Court Orders that were to follow.

Every visit was miserable and getting Sam ready in time to be picked up was a nightmare. Joanne felt guilty about making Sam go and Sam hated going. He sobbed, he pleaded and he ran upstairs and hid in Joanne and Chris's bed.

Joanne sat on the bed and had tried to explain to Sam that, as a family, they had no choice; Sam had been ordered to go on contact visits: that was what the Court had decreed.

Gregory would pull his car up at the end of Joanne and Chris's driveway and sounded the car horn. Joanne couldn't bring herself to take Sam out to Gregory's car. To her it felt as though she was betraying Sam's trust in her. Instead, Chris had the job of leading Sam down the driveway, but at the end of the driveway Chris stopped and waited for Gregory to try to persuade Sam into the car.

Joanne watched from the hall window. She felt sick inside and powerless: unable to prevent Sam from having to go through this. She hung onto Springer's collar as he scratched at the front door, trying to follow Sam. She watched through the window as Sam put out his arms, feet firmly on the ground and refused to get into Gregory's car. Gregory tried to force Sam to get in. Joanne turned away, *what a bastard*, Joanne thought, *how can he do that?*

Joanne could not watch anymore, she leaned her back against the wall, her eyes tight shut and slowly slid down to the floor and sat there, her face buried in her hands. She could hear Sam's protests and tears rolled down her face while Springer fussed around her, not understanding what was going on.

Joanne felt a little tug at her skirt. It was Alex.

"Where's Sam going to Mum . . . Mum why does he have to go if he doesn't want to?" but all Joanne could reply was,

"Because it's the law!"

Joanne pulled Alex into her arms and hugged him close to her; there was no way that she would ever let Alex go through what Sam was suffering.

While comforting Alex, Joanne listened to what was going on outside. She could hear Michael, who lived on the opposite side of the road, come over to Gregory's car. Michael was a good neighbour and was always ready to help. She could hear him ask:

"Sam . . . Sam are you ok? Do you want some help here?"

Gregory responded in anger . . .

"It's non of your bloody business! Get lost!"

Joanne had heard all that she could bare. She hugged Alex, while with her other hand she ran her fingers through Springer's soft fur. He was a lovely dog, so good-natured and such a good friend to Sam.

That evening when Sam was returned home at six, there was a timid knock at the door. Joanne, Chris and Alex rushed to greet him, but as Sam came into the house Joanne could smell something was not quite right.

"Alex, go and wait in the sitting room for us and we'll all come and join you, we'll have a snuggle up and watch a movie together . . ."

Alex dutifully disappeared. Joanne gave Sam a hug and suddenly realised that his clothes were covered in urine. Sam pulled a small car out of his soggy pocket,

"I brought this for Alex," he said, "a present."

"You are so kind Sam, but you don't have to bring back presents. You're home! Lets get these clothes off you, have a lovely hot bubble bath, then watch a movie. Are you hungry, would you like something to eat?"

Sam shook his head. He looked very pale and there seemed a sort of numbness about him, as though he couldn't really speak. He pulled some crushed wild flowers out of his shirt pocket,

"And these are for you mum."

Joanne hugged Sam again, then she helped him remove his wet clothes and run a bubble bath for him. Joanne threw Sam's clothes into the washer; they smelt rancid, not just of urine, but generally of unwashed clothes. What had happened, that had so frightened this little boy that, at nearly six years old, he had wet himself?

Joanne talked to friends who had seen Sam and Gregory together. They always reported back that Sam seemed okay with Gregory, nothing out of the ordinary. How was it then that Gregory could put on one face in public, pretending that everything was normal and then, afterwards, he had done something bad enough to make Sam wet himself?

The next Sunday evening Sam was dropped off at the end of the drive. Joanne heard the car draw up and, looking out of the hall window, was delighted to see Sam getting out of the car. As soon as Sam had shut the car door, Gregory put his foot down hard on the accelerator and sped off. Sam walked up the driveway and Joanne and Chris ran out to greet him.

"Hey Sam! Great to have you home! How did it go?" asked Joanne, then, as she bent down to kiss him, she paused,

"Wow Sam . . . is that petrol I can smell?"

"Oh . . . sorry mum . . . he told me to fill up the car mum . . . we were at the petrol station and Gregory told me to fill up the car while he went into the shop for something. But then it all splashed back at me, sorry mum, I couldn't help it, it went all over me . . ."

Sam's trousers and shirt were drenched. Chris and Joanne looked at each other; the same thoughts went through their minds. They quickly got Sam into a bath and then into clean pyjamas.

Over the next few days it took Joanne three or four separate washing cycles to get the smell of petrol from Sam's clothes and all the time Joanne kept trying to figure out what was going on in Gregory's mind, what *was* he doing?

It seemed that every time Sam came back home; there was always something that had gone awry.

At every weekend visit it seemed Gregory was determined to make life as difficult and miserable as possible. Sometimes Sam was delivered back home as late as ten in the evening, tired, not having done his homework, not having had any supper and with only half the clothes he was sent away with. Sometimes Sam was dropped off early. It was not possible for Joanne and Chris to plan a Sunday outing with Alex because they never knew when Sam might be returned home. Sometimes Sam was not brought home at all and Chris and Joanne spent the evening 'phoning people to see where Sam might be. On some occasions it was several days later that Sam was returned to them, having missed two or three days of school.

Sam never talked much about his visits to Gregory, but at bedtime when Joanne came to kiss him good night, sometimes he would grumble, mumbling to himself,

"Why do I have to be locked in the hotel room while Gregory goes out? I wouldn't get into trouble, I'd just sit and watch TV; what was the problem with that? Why should I be dragged along to meet builders in the country and stand outside in the cold for hours? I tried to get into the house to get my jacket, but the door was locked. *And* he forgets to give me food . . ."

Sam particularly hated having to clean out Gregory's car. The interior was littered with rotting food and half eaten sandwiches hanging out of their plastic packets, discarded drink cans, their now dried up contents soaked into the carpet, half drunk bottles of Lucozade and sweetie packets with melted chocolate oozing out. The smell made Sam feel sick.

Sam was worried about his homework, too. He had not been allowed to collect it from his room before being told to get into the car to return home to Joanne. He had tried to do his homework, but Gregory had told him that there wasn't time for that; there were more important things to do.

When Joanne asked Sam why he had come home without his socks or pants, he said that it was just that he couldn't find them in his room when he woke up in the morning, so he just wore a shirt and trousers. Sam was really sorry about not being able to find his jacket; he knew that clothes were expensive and he didn't want his mother to be upset. He knew the family couldn't afford to keep on buying him new ones.

As time went on, the nights became more disturbed. Joanne was woken by the sound of sobbing and found Sam sitting bolt upright in bed, eyes wide open but not seeing anything and shouting between sobs. Joanne couldn't hold or hug him, he was too rigid and so she stroked his back and tried to sooth him. She tried to understand what he was dreaming about, but apart from what sounded like "No!" and "Stop!" she could not make out much. It took twenty minutes or so before she could get Sam settled back down the bed.

The next day Sam would not remember what had happened in the night, nor did he remember Joanne being with him. Amazingly, Alex slept through the crying. Joanne supposed he had got used to it and the noise no longer disturbed his sleep. Sam also started to wet his bed at night, so Joanne had to buy the biggest pull-up disposable night pants she could find, to try and save the bedding from getting too ruined.

The next blow was that Sam's school reported that Sam was not progressing. He had appeared to be talented when he first joined the school, but he had changed from a lively, confident little boy, to a little boy who sat in class in a daydream, as if he was in another world. He was not keeping up with his classmates and seemed to have forgotten even what he had learnt in the previous year. Sam had fallen well behind his peers, nearly a year behind and the school thought that he should be assessed as to what his difficulties might be.

The headmistress suggested that Sam should see a child therapist sometimes used by the school. Her name was Susan Charmers who lived locally and she was very experienced in helping children in difficult circumstances.

Susan held her sessions at her home. She had a small stone, terraced house in a quiet cul-de-sac, with a pretty paved path leading to the front door.

When Susan greeted them at the door, she had short wavy brown hair and wore a full skirt and blousy top which made her small frame look plumper than she really was. She had a jolly and motherly manner about her that made Joanne and Sam feel at ease.

She led the way into her cosy sitting room and smiled at Sam as she patted the settee, inviting him to sit next to her. She suggested to Joanne that she should go into the kitchen and make herself a cup of tea.

Joanne made her way to the small kitchen. Sure enough, the table had been laid with a flowery tablecloth, in the middle of which was a pretty china teapot and three matching mugs with milk and sugar and a tin of assorted biscuits.

About an hour later Susan and Sam emerged looking very relaxed together, Sam was still eagerly chatting, telling her about Springer and Alex.

"Sam, can you swop places with your mum now? I just want to have a quick chat with her and you can help yourself to the biscuits on the kitchen table. I'll only be a minute or two."

With that, Susan showed Joanne into her sitting room. She asked Joanne to briefly outline what she regarded as the problem. She had already received some background notes from the headmistress, but she wanted to hear Joanne's perspective.

Susan told Joanne that she thought Sam was a delightful little boy and thanked them both for coming to see her and that she would write with some suggestions.

A report duly arrived some days later. Susan wrote that the most important thing was to focus on Sam and to help him regain his confidence in order to grow and develop emotionally, socially and academically. Susan suggested that Sam should go to see her once a week to talk about any problems that he had at school, or home or during his visits to Gregory. She enjoyed her initial meeting with Sam and suggested that visits to Gregory were reduced to one day every other weekend and only to gradually increase visits to allow Sam to acclimatise over time.

A further letter arrived a week later. Susan wrote to Joanne saying that Gregory had clearly not liked her suggestions! She had emphasised to Gregory that, in her work with children, it was always the needs of the child that were uppermost in her mind. Her advice in her report was to focus on *Sam's* needs. She concluded that, with regret, she must withdraw from the consultation but she would be happy to give names and telephone numbers of other therapists who might be able to help Sam.

What had Gregory written to Susan? What did he say to make her withdraw her assistance so abruptly? He must have been very forthright. But wasn't that Gregory all over? Things had to be done *his* way. His view was that Sam was merely a child and should be told what to do: one didn't ask a *child* what he wanted or did not want.

Gregory then decided to take matters into his own hands and started collecting Sam from school for his weekend visit, rather than from outside home. There was no Court agreement that Sam should be collected from school, Gregory just decided to do it.

He also changed his mind as to which weekend he wanted to have contact with Sam. The constant changing of schedule really upset Sam; he liked to go home after school. He didn't want to go straight from school to Gregory's house. He wanted to change into his home clothes and pick up his favourite toys. Sam was upset that he couldn't plan weekends with his friends, because he never knew where he was going to be. When he was invited to go to his friend's house Gregory refused to let him go. Sam wanted to go to his friend's parties, but Gregory made it clear to Sam that his contact visits were to see Gregory, not go to friend's birthday parties. What was more, Sam did not like going to Gregory's house in the country; he didn't know anyone there and anyway, he would only be left on his own to look after himself.

Then Sam started wetting himself in class. Instead of asking to be excused to go to the toilet, he just sat there in a pool of urine. Matron said that it always happened on a Friday. She patiently provided Sam with clean clothes from the 'lost property' cupboard and popped his wet shorts and pants in a polythene bag in Sam's satchel. Then, even worse, Sam's classmates started to call him "Smelly".

Gregory arranged a meeting with the headmistress and told her that Joanne was turning the boy against him. He succeeded in intimidating her and insisted that it was her duty to encourage Sam in his contact visits.

Sam's teachers became more and more concerned, but nobody dared to say, or do, anything, for fear of being accused of obstructing what the Court had ordered.

One afternoon Joanne got a 'phone call from Sam's form teacher:

"Mrs Parry, it's Sam's teacher; there is no need to worry, but I thought I should let you know that Mr Franks picked up Sam a few minutes ago. He said that they had an early train to catch and he needed to take Sam out of school earlier than usual."

"*He did what!*" exclaimed Joanne, "But that's ridiculous! Sam is meant to be with *us* this weekend!"

"I'm really sorry Mrs Parry, but the school is obliged to go along with reasonable wishes of the parents. I just didn't want you to make the trip to school and then find that Sam was not here. You say it's not his weekend?"

"That's right! He can't just take Sam out of school when he fancies, especially when Sam is meant to be with us."

There was a pause while Sam's teacher considered the predicament,

"Maybe the thing to do is to let us have a copy of the latest Court Order that lists the weekends Sam is meant to be with Mr Franks. We can't of course *stop* Mr Franks coming to the school, but we could possibly let you know when he arrives and I think in future we could possibly request that he waits until the end of the school day."

"Well," said Joanne resignedly, "Yes, that would be very helpful. I'll let you have a copy of the Court Order on Monday; but it's this sort of thing that upsets Sam; it affects his schoolwork, he just doesn't know what he's doing from one weekend to the next. It's all so disruptive!"

Two weeks later Joanne got another call from Sam's form teacher,

"Mrs Parry, I just thought to let you know that Mr Franks has arrived at school early to collect Sam. We appreciate that it is not his weekend to have Sam and we have asked Mr Franks to wait in the main hallway until school is finished. He is sitting outside the headmistress's room."

"Oh! Right! Thank you. Should I come and collect Sam now? It's only just three o'clock."

"I think on this occasion you should come straight to Sam's classroom. Use the back entrance to the school. By the time you arrive it will be nearly the end of the school day and I can let you have Sam as soon as you arrive," she sounded a bit self-conscious, "I'll see you later!" she said and abruptly rang off.

Sam's form teacher was watching for Joanne through the classroom window. As soon as she saw Joanne approaching the classroom, she ushered Sam from his desk, with jacket and homework bag and delivered him safely into Joanne's arms.

After that episode, Joanne thought it was prudent to arrive fifteen or twenty minutes early at Sam's school and she brought a magazine to read to pass the time while Alex had a nap in his pushchair. Sometimes she didn't get the chance to read because Alex liked to climb on the playground climbing-frame and she needed to keep a careful watch on him in case he was too adventurous!

Today, as she pushed Alex in his pushchair towards the front door of the school, she heard someone knocking on the window above her. Joanne looked up and saw a teacher motion to Joanne to go round the back. As Joanne got to the back door, Sam's form teacher was already waiting for her. Joanne was ushered inside with Alex and told to wait in the children's cloakroom. Meanwhile, Sam's teacher quietly went back into the classroom, took Sam's hand and led him out. She then thrust Sam's jacket and school bag into Joanne's arms.

"Matron has given Sam some clean shorts and pants, the wet ones are in his bag." She patted Sam's head and hurriedly steered them all outside.

Joanne and Chris had tried writing letters to Gregory explaining that children need routine; something they could rely on; a definite schedule to make them feel secure in that they should know what they were doing from one day to the next. It was difficult to know if Gregory didn't stick to the dates listed in the Court Order intentionally to mess everyone about, or if it was in his own self-interest: it just suited him better. Maybe it was a bit of both, but that didn't help Sam.

No sooner had Joanne thought that she had mastered one hurdle, Gregory found her another one.

The next Friday when Joanne arrived at school to collect Sam, she found his teacher looking most perplexed,

"Sam's gone with Fiona!"

"Gone with Fiona? What do you mean?"

"She said that she was helping you out! She said you couldn't make it or something and that Sam needed to be picked up early. She left about twenty minutes ago!"

Fiona? What was Fiona doing collecting Sam on a Friday! She often helped Joanne out, collecting Sam from school on the days Joanne worked, Monday to Thursday, but *never* on a Friday.

Sam's teacher looked more and more concerned as she saw the horror spread over Joanne's face.

"I'm really sorry Joanne! We are so used to Fiona collecting Sam that we didn't think to question it!"

"Don't worry, it's not your fault! Did you say about twenty minutes ago?"

"Yes. You'd better hurry!"

Joanne's heart was beating frantically. Which way would Fiona have gone? By bus, maybe? Surely she wouldn't walk; it would be too far for Sam to walk all the way. But which route? By now they must be nearly at Gregory's house.

Joanne hurriedly carried Alex to her parked car. She briskly shoved the pushchair into the boot of the car and plonked Alex in his baby chair on the back seat and strapped him in as quickly as she could. Then turned on the engine and sped off as fast as she dared. The last thing she needed was the police to stop her for speeding.

"Mummy, where are we going?" asked Alex; confused that Joanne should be in such a hurry.

"We're going to get Sam back and we have to hurry! Please Alex, please be a good little boy and sit quietly, please help me look for Sam! He'll be with Fiona, walking somewhere, we've got to find him!"

Joanne overtook traffic where she could and rushed through traffic lights. There were children everywhere coming home from school. Joanne peered at each little fair-haired boy walking with an adult, at the same time trying to keep her eye on the road.

As Joanne drove the car into Gregory's road her heart sank. She'd not seen Sam and Fiona. She'd looked on both sides of the road; her eyes had scanned the pavements and every crossing. Maybe Fiona had already dropped Sam off at Gregory's. Maybe she was too late.

Joanne slowed down the car and was about to turn around and go back home when she saw two figures turn into the road. It was Sam and Fiona! Sam was eating an ice cream and obviously in deep conversation with Fiona who walked attentively next to him. So that's why she had missed them, they must have stopped at the local newsagents on the way.

Joanne accelerated the car towards them, drew up and hastily wound down the car window.

"Fiona! What are you doing? Sam is meant to be with *me* this weekend!"

"Oh Joanne! Oh no! Joanne I'm so, so, sorry! I got a message at work that you couldn't pick up Sam from School and that it was Gregory's weekend and that I was to take Sam to Gregory's."

"But, that's rubbish! I would *never* ask you to take Sam to Gregory's!"

"The message said that arrangements had changed and it would help you out if I could collect Sam and bring him here. I *thought* it was odd that you should ask me to take Sam to Gregory's. I didn't think to ask at the desk who left the message. If they had said a man, I suppose I would have questioned it. I just didn't think. I'm so sorry luv!"

"Well Sam!" said Fiona, guiding Sam to the passenger door, "you'd better get in the car and get home quick! I'll be getting back to the hotel, I've still got some work to do before I'm finished for the day."

φ

It was Friday a typical February night; cold and drizzling as Joanne drove the car to collect Chris from the local train station. Sam was spending half term with Gregory and was not due back until Sunday. Alex was in the back of the car, asleep in his car seat, snug in his pyjamas and his warm fleece dressing gown.

Joanne was looking forward to hearing how Chris had got on helping out a fellow surgeon in Birmingham. She managed to park next to the station entrance and could see the station steps and people making their way, holding their coats around them, some with their umbrellas up, others holding newspapers or whatever was to hand against the persistent drizzle. She looked eagerly for Chris, then she recognised his long coat and black umbrella and she flashed the car lights to get his attention.

Chris got in the car next to Joanne, his coat dripping wet. He kissed her, then lent over the back of his seat to peep at Alex, still fast asleep.

As they drove home Joanne listened eagerly as Chris told her the events of the day, there had been some challenging cases to deal with and Chris was full of enthusiasm. Chris and Joanne planned to set up a practice together and Joanne was keen to learn as much as she could about his work and the way he liked to work.

It was nine o'clock and dark as Joanne backed the car into the driveway. The street lamps shed a soft light to show the way.

As she parked the car she thought she saw a figure crouched among the flowerpots near the front door, but then dismissed it from her mind as not being very likely and probably just the shadows. But as Joanne and Chris got out of the car a little figure ran up to them. It was Sam! He was wet and shivering, his T-shirt clung to his small frame and his trousers legs were stuffed in the wellingtons he was wearing.

"Sam!" Joanne called to him, "What are you doing here . . . its wonderful to see you . . . but . . . how long have you been here . . . what happened?"

Sam explained that Gregory had dropped him off at the end of the road and left him there to make his way to the house. Joanne looked across at Chris and Chris shook his head,

"Incredible,' he muttered as he went back into the car to get Alex.

Joanne thought back. She had set off for the station at just after seven . . . Sam could have been there an hour or more. No matter, she hugged him, then unlocked the front door and let him inside. He was cold. She sat him down on the hall stairs and helped him take off his wellingtons. Joanne felt his cold feet; no socks again, he must be frozen!

"Well its wonderful to have you back," Joanne said cheerily, "lets have a hot bath, something to eat and maybe a story."

It was outrageous that Gregory could go to Court, claim how much he wanted to see this little boy and then just dump him in the road on a cold wet night. Anything could have happened to him. Gregory hadn't even checked if Chris and Joanne were away for the weekend . . .

This time Joanne really had had enough of Gregory's pretences of caring for Sam. She decided to go to Court on Monday morning and see the Judge of the day and try and get someone to see sense. After all, if Gregory could go to Court and make an application without giving her notice, then she was going to see if she could do the same.

Monday came. Chris went off as usual to the hospital and Joanne ordered a taxi. There was no way she would be able to park their car near the Courts, she had Alex to care for and goodness knows how long she would have to wait before she was seen by a Judge. She would just have to wait her turn in the queue.

Joanne had heard that some Judges were more amenable than others and you needed to look at the list of the day to see which Judge was allocated to hear any unlisted cases.

Joanne walked up the imposing Victorian stone steps to the large wooden gates at the entrance to the Courts. She carried Alex on her left hip, her arm around his waist and with her other hand she held onto Sam. She took a deep breath as she entered the hall, it felt chilled; there was not much light in the old building and the stone floors gave it an austere atmosphere. They approached the old mahogany reception desk, where three receptionists were giving people directions and trying to assist with enquiries.

There was a list of Judges who were sitting that day, posted to one side of the desk. Joanne looked through the names but they didn't mean anything to her. She looked at the three attendants. Which one looked the most likely to be sympathetic to her request? One of the lady attendants looked as though she was from Africa, a big mamma type, she seemed to be the friendliest looking of the three.

"I wonder, please, if you can help me . . . it's difficult to explain . . . my son Sam here," Joanne said motioning to Sam who was clinging tightly to her hand, "is very distressed at having to go on contact visits and I wondered if you could help me identify which of the Judges are the most likely to be sympathetic on a matter such as this?"

The big mamma looked first at Joanne, then at the two little boys, then back at the list of Judges.

"Well", she pondered, considering the list, "you may hit lucky today, no promises . . . but Judge Butterman is on today and she is a very experienced Judge in family matters."

The attendant directed Joanne to walk down the long hall to the end and follow the signs to Court forty-five. Joanne dutifully walked down the cold marble hallway, the sound of her heels clicking on the hard floor echoed off the cold stone walls around them. Large portraits of Judges hung on the walls, in their elaborate gold frames and seemed to look down at them as they walked by. Joanne followed the old signs with gold painted arrows and numbers on wooded plaques saying 'Court 30—50' directing her down a dark stone corridor until eventually she came out into a larger hallway with a row of doors and the Court numbers painted in gold over them. Joanne walked down the hallway until she reached Court number forty-five. There was an old wooden table, which served as a desk and hard wooden benches to sit on. Joanne was feeling the strain from carrying Alex so far and was about to sit down on one of the benches when a middle-aged clerk in a black suit and flowing black gown approached her. The clerk looked kind enough as she asked Joanne's name and added it to the list. She then looked at Sam and Alex and said to Joanne:

"You can't take children into the Courts you know!"

Joanne knew that, but what else was she meant to do? She needed the Judge to see Sam, to understand what he was going through, she had to do something different, to make the Judge sit up and listen. Judges were making Court orders about a little boy they had never met, Sam was just a name on a list, they didn't know how he felt, whether he was timid or bullish, sensitive or hard. Had they asked themselves if this little boy was in need of nurture and shelter?

At last it was Joanne's turn to go into Court, this was now the twenty fifth Court hearing. Joanne watched the previous party stroll out through the Court doors, their heads bowed, exchanging opinions in lowered voices. The clerk motioned to Joanne to follow her into a small anti-chamber just outside the official Court room door and told her to sit there on the bench with her two boys, while the clerk went in to Court to have a word with the Judge.

A few minutes later, the clerk re-appeared.

"You are to go into Court now and a welfare officer will look after the children and entertain them.

Joanne left Alex and Sam with the clerk and entered the Courtroom. Judge Butterman sat behind a tall bench set on a raised platform. Her clerk stood by a table, which served as a desk at the foot of the platform. Judge Butterman looked up as Joanne entered the room, her greying hair tied back in a bun. She looked slim and tall behind the large bench. There were rows of benches facing the judge and the clerk motioned to Joanne to sit at the front.

Judge Butterman invited Joanne to speak. Joanne stood up and, calming herself, she did her best to give the facts of the case slowly and clearly and as unemotionally as possible. She tried to describe the ordeal that Sam was being put through on his contact visits. The Judge listened carefully and seemed to take in the seriousness of the situation. She seemed particularly concerned when Joanne described Sam's latest visit to Gregory.

She then told her clerk to contact Mrs Rex, the senior Court welfare officer and asked her to interview Sam. Judge Butterman explained to Joanne that Mrs Rex was very kind and experienced and would give an accurate report of Sam's thoughts and feelings. Judge Butterman then told Joanne to take a seat outside the Court and that, after Sam had been interviewed, Joanne would be brought back into Court to hear Mrs Rex's report.

About an hour and a half later Joanne was ordered back into Court. Joanne hoped that Mrs Rex had asked the right questions and heard from Sam what was upsetting him.

Mrs Rex's view was that Sam *was* unhappy on these visits and that they should be limited.

Limited! That did not address the problem. Gregory was abusing this little boy and probably his only motive was to cause Joanne anguish.

Judge Butterman ordered no contact for two weeks to let Sam settle down and then to resume contact, starting with alternate Saturdays for two months and Sam to be brought back home by six in the evening. Then contact was to be increased to Saturday and Sunday and again Sam to be returned home by six.

Going home in the taxi with Sam and Alex sitting either side of her, Joanne felt that at least the Judge had listened to her, but she felt disappointed and low. It was clear that the rules were that there had to be contact visits, no matter how miserable they were for Sam.

No sooner had the new Court Order been sent to Gregory, but Gregory was back in Court getting the Order reversed. Joanne was ordered to appear in two weeks time, this time before Judge Walker.

The day was bright and sunny as Joanne arrived at the grand entrance to the Courts. She stepped out of the taxi onto the pavement, the sunlight warm on her face as she juggled with her black computer bag and handbag to find the money to pay the taxi driver. Then she turned and walked up the large stone steps and through the entrance to the Courts. Here it was cold and airless.

Huge grey stone walls bordered the old hall. The only windows were high up near the vaulted roof. A bit like a cathedral, thought Joanne, but here it was soulless.

Two security guards eyed her as she approached. One stepped forward and commanded,

"Put your bags on here please, including your 'phone."

Joanne duly put her bags on the conveyor belt then walked towards the metal detector that everyone had to walk through, bit like the airport, she thought to herself, trying to make light of the tension she felt inside her. As Joanne walked through, it made a terrible screech. She had told herself that this would happen to prepare herself for the embarrassment, but she still felt awkward about it.

A woman security guard approached Joanne,

"It's possibly the heels of your shoes!" she said curtly. Joanne removed her high heels, placed them on the conveyor belt and walked through the metal detector again. It screeched again. This was just great! You dressed in a black suit and tried to look ultra smart and business like and then they slowly unclothe you!

"Maybe it's your belt!" the woman security guard suggested resignedly, "Ok you can collect your things and go through. Which Court are you in?"

"I was told Court twelve, West Wing I think?"

"Yes. Follow the hallway to the end and then turn left. You'll see it sign-posted."

Joanne recovered her shoes, picked up her bags and, now feeling slightly disconcerted and less confident, she made her way down the imposing hall and turned left as she had been directed. She pushed through the heavy wooden swing doors that lead into a smaller hallway. There were Court doors on the right and opposite each Court door was a table and benches where people dressed in black sat dutifully. Some talked in hushed tones, their papers neatly stacked on the tables. Some made anxious notes as they sipped coffee from paper cups.

Joanne walked down the hallway until she came to Court number twelve and found herself space on the bench outside. She laid her computer bag and handbag on the table in front of her, like a protective barrier between her and the Court. She felt alone and wished Chris could have been with her, but he was at the hospital. The case had dragged on for so long now that the Hospital was getting impatient with the amount of time Chris had taken off work to support Joanne in Court. One minute Joanne felt nervous about what would happen in Court, the next minute she felt a surge of determination. She was here for Sam, here to protect her family.

Ushers walked up and down the hallway, their long black flowing robes billowing out behind them. One of them approached Joanne with a list of the day's cases on a clipboard.

"Are you here for Court twelve?" she demanded.

Joanne nodded and stood up to show respect:

"Yes I am."

"Your name please?"

"Joanne, Joanne Parry."

"Case of Parry and Franks?"

"Yes, that's right!"

"Okay, stay here please. You're listed for ten thirty. I'll call you before Court begins. Court always starts on time!"

"Thank you!" said Joanne nervously and sat down again.

At ten twenty-eight, the usher stood outside Court twelve and announced loudly.

"Case of Parry and Franks!"

Joanne stood up and gathered her things.

"Joanne Parry?" asked the usher. Joanne nodded grimly, "follow me!" she instructed and turned and led Joanne through the Court door.

"Sit along here" she directed and pointed to the end of the bench some four rows back from the front of the Court.

Joanne walked along side the bench to the end and sat down. She placed her computer bag in front of her on the desk and her handbag next to her on the bench, making sure that her mobile 'phone inside her handbag was switched to silent. Having settled herself down, she sat up and looked around her. There was Judge's usual raised bench with tall red leather padded back and a large coat of arms high on the wall above with some Latin inscription underneath, which Joanne couldn't quite make out. Then she saw Gregory was already seated on the front row of benches, in front of the Judge's bench, his papers and books already laid out in front of him. Joanne suddenly felt cold and slightly shaky. Once again Gregory had the upper hand; he was already in Court and he was prepared. No doubt he had already had a chat with the Judge to put him in the picture. You were meant to go in to Court together, not one sneak in before the other. Joanne felt like an outsider in unknown territory.

At one side of the Judge's bench there was a small desk where a clerk sat dressed in her black suit and gown, her dark hair tied back neatly with a ribbon. So the clerk had let Gregory into Court first.

"All rise!" The clerk suddenly announced. Judge Walker swaggered into the room with his red gown flowing about him and took his seat at his lofty bench. The clerk then gathered up some papers off her desk and carried them over to Joanne. She placed them in front of her, then turned and went back to her seat. Joanne stared down at bundle of A4 typed sheets. Open-mouthed, she flicked through the pages. There looked to be at least twenty or thirty to read. How could she do that in such a short time and prepare a response? This was typical of Gregory! Always the criminal law barrister: he bent the rules to his advantage.

Joanne had been advised to do things by the book. She was told to prepare her papers before going to Court, to serve them on Gregory in advance of the hearing date, to allow Gregory time to make his response and then everyone's papers were to be served to the Court together. But Gregory had his own agenda; he didn't serve *his* papers! Instead, *he* was allowed to hand his papers to Joanne *at* the Court. Gregory could do that and he did.

Joanne braced herself. She stood up and addressed Judge Walker.

"My Lord! I have only *just* been handed Mr Frank's papers and I have not had the chance to get legal advice. I am representing myself, with no legal background. Please may I be given time to get advice?"

The Judge grudgingly lifted his head. He looked at her and said:

"Well . . . you have the papers *now*! I'll give you some time to read them . . . in the meantime perhaps Mr Franks would be good enough to put his case to me."

Gregory rose to his feet enthusiastically, "My Lord! Yes indeed! Thank you!" he said bowing.

Gregory had such a pompous way of addressing the Judge and such a dismissive way of referring to Joanne as though she was the lowest form of life. Gregory declared that Joanne exaggerated the way Sam felt. Sam, he said, was happy on his visits to him; Sam was so happy that sometimes he didn't even want to go back home to his mum! Sam's mother was simply putting him up to telling lies to the welfare officer. Gregory said that it was *Joanne* who did not want Sam to go on visits and that was where the problem lay. It was not a case of Sam not wanting to go on the visits.

As Joanne listened she could not believe how Gregory could sweep all those unhappy incidents under the carpet and pretend that they never happened. Whatever Gregory said, Judge Walker revered it as the gospel truth, nodding in sympathy and understanding. However, when Joanne spoke, it seemed to Joanne that her words were automatically regarded as lies, after all, she was merely a woman!

So Judge Walker reversed the ruling by Judge Butterman to gently ease Sam back into contact visits with Gregory!

The 'hearing' was a farce! Did anyone *hear* anything except what Mr Gregory Franks, the barrister, said?

Joanne was told by the clerk to rise; everyone bowed to the Judge and left the Court. Everyone, that is, except Gregory. He stayed behind. No doubt for a chat with the Judge and his clerk.

The system was just *so* one sided it was *unbelievable*. Gregory was a criminal law barrister, but he had friends in family law who would look up and research that side of things for him without charge. By contrast, Chris and Joanne had to spend hours researching in the law libraries, or seeking advice at the Citizens' Advice Bureau. They had little money to spare and they certainly couldn't afford solicitors: they all cost so much money and Chris's, mostly National Health Service salary did not go very far.

Joanne had taken some advice from the solicitors at the local Citizens' Advice Bureau, but was exasperated to find that each solicitor had a different idea. First Joanne was advised to dress in black, not to show any bare flesh: no low necklines or short skirts. Tie her hair back, not wear any make-up. In other words, look as nun-like as possible. Then she was told to wear make-up and short skirts. But nothing seemed to get the attention of the Judges; nobody seemed to listen to her. The best result she could get was when the Judge actually thought she might be cold in her skimpy attire and offered her a seat near to the radiator!

Finally, Joanne was lucky to meet Elizabeth at the Citizen's Advice Bureau. Elizabeth was a young and enthusiastic solicitor who was doing her bit of charity work by advising people for free, two days a week. Elizabeth didn't look like the usual formal solicitor. She was tall and pretty, with straight, blond, shoulder length hair. She preferred to dress informally; a simple blouse and skirt with flat shoes to compensate for her height. Elizabeth was sympathetic; she too had a young son and when she heard Sam's story she was amazed and could not believe what this family was going through.

Elizabeth did her best to furnish Chris and Joanne with the relevant forms they needed to make applications to the Court. She taught Joanne how to style her documents, how to prepare her statements and how to put her case forward.

But she also warned Joanne that the Courts were a man's world. Women were only tolerated there. The Judges and barristers had their own network that was difficult to penetrate. The bottom line was that Joanne was merely a woman!

"What I don't understand," said Joanne to Elizabeth, "is that, if a child is unhappy on visits to his father, then why does he have to be put through the misery? The Children's Act states that the wishes and feeling of the child should be taken into account. But, in Sam's case, his wishes and feelings are totally ignored! And, why is it so unheard of to have a DNA test? Sam looks nothing like Gregory. Sam was born through IVF. What if the clinic made a mistake?"

"It doesn't make any difference," sighed an exasperated Elizabeth. "The Children's Act of 1991 states that whoever the 'parents' were at the time of birth remain the parents and the child should have access to both parents."

"But surely that's the point! Sam was born in 1990—he is not affected by the Act."

"The Judges will not even *entertain* such an idea!"

"Why not?"

"Because they won't! Simple as that! You mention such a notion and they will jump down your throat. Damn you as the most evil woman of all time!"

"How archaic! I still don't understand why Sam should be held to that Act if he was born *before* the Act. Can't we get a barrister to look it up and find out?"

"Joanne, it's a waste of time. Believe me! No barrister is going to put that before a Judge. What's more, you are up against a barrister, not a cat in Hell's chance; they all stick together."

"But what about a DNA test?"

"Same! Not a chance!"

"Funny you should say that . . . when Chris and I first asked for a DNA test to be done on Sam, because Sam looked nothing like Gregory, the Judge went ballistic! Said he would not hear of such a thing. Dismissed the idea completely. Said that the matter should never be raised again! What is wrong with these people? Which planet are they from?"

φ

Patrick was Sam's godfather and he had also been Gregory's best man. Patricks's family ran a private Bank and he too had been a barrister. In fact, when Joanne thought about it, all Gregory's friends were barristers, except one who was a solicitor. Patrick had decided some years ago to leave the Bar. He thought that its influence was beginning to rub off on him and an opportunity came up for him to take over his father's business. Patrick was a good godfather and kept in touch with Sam. He began to get uneasy about the increasing number of Court hearings and how this must be affecting Sam. He decided to 'phone Joanne,

"Joanne! It's Patrick, Patrick Church. I thought I'd give you guys a call and see how you're doing?"

"Patrick! How nice to hear from you!"

"To be honest, Joanne, I'm calling because I'm concerned about Sam! Can you update me a bit?"

Joanne gave him a brief account of what had happened so far.

"Maybe I should take Sam out for a good lunch somewhere and see how the little chap is bearing up. If that's all right with you, Joanne?"

"I'd be delighted, Patrick. It's most kind of you to take an interest. I'll get Sam to the 'phone and you can arrange something between you."

Sam found it easy to talk to Patrick. He found him fatherly and caring. Patrick had a son a little younger than Sam and was used to talking to children.

When Patrick brought Sam back home. Joanne and Chris invited Patrick to sit and have a glass of wine with them.

Making sure that Sam was out of earshot and playing upstairs with Alex, Patrick came straight to the point.

"I'm *horrified! Shocked* at the way this case is being handled. Sam is obviously *greatly* distressed going on these contact visits, it just isn't right. There's something seriously wrong here. Can you show me some Court papers on the case?"

Chris fetched his computer, placed it on the dining table and opened up the files for Patrick to peruse with him.

"There's rather a lot I'm afraid!" apologised Chris. Patrick peered at the screen in disbelief; there were just so many Court Orders to go through.

"Would you mind if I take a copy of them away to read?"

"Not at all, we'd be delighted for your help. Just tell me which ones you'd like to take and I'll print them out for you."

A week later Patrick called Joanne.

"I've read all I need to read on Sam's case. I'm quite sickened. I really don't *want* to get involved, but I do *feel* that, for Sam's sake, I *must* and *should* give some input here. Would you be happy for me to make a statement for Court as Sam's god-father?"

"That would be tremendous of you Patrick! We have a hearing coming up shortly and with your position as god-father and ex-barrister, I am sure that it can only be a help."

"I'll have to get a solicitor to look over my statement. I'm a bit rusty at this now-a-days, but I will certainly prepare my statement and although I do not intend to go into Court, unless called, I will accompany you all and sit outside the Courtroom in case I'm needed. I have to say Joanne, that I think Gregory has gone off the rails somewhat. I think Criminal Law can rub off on you after a bit and I think that that is what has happened here. Gregory's changed. Definitely changed. Not the man I used to know at all."

So at the fifty-sixth Court hearing, the Judge decided that he was now in an impossible position. On the one hand he had Gregory, a barrister, demanding his right to see the child. On the other hand he had the mother describing the distress being caused to her son by miserable incidents during contact visits. The Judge now also had Sam's godfather's statement. So, finally, he decided to defer the case to the Official Solicitor, whose role was to represent the rights of children.

The Official Solicitor's office had undergone many changes and the Judge had not caught up with the fact that it had been renamed. Its latest name was CAFCASS. That stood for Children and Family Court Advisory and Support Service. CAFCASS would allocate an officer to assess Sam's case, to understand Sam's wishes and make recommendations to the Court that were thought to be in his best interest.

The officer in this case was a Miss Graves: a dumpy creature in ill-fitting clothes more suited to someone ten years older. Her short, straight, mousey hair, which looked as though it needed a shampoo, said to the world that she didn't care what she looked like. But she had *authority*! Or was it power?

Gregory took his usual attitude that he was the most important person in the world. He made it clear to the poor unsuspecting Miss Graves that he was so busy, so important and in such demand by the Courts, that the only time he could be interviewed was at a weekend and at his home!

Like a mouse hypnotized by a snake writhing and darting his eyes at her, Miss Graves was completely taken in by Gregory's story that he desperately wanted contact with the child. He lectured Miss Graves: the law ensured that each child was *made* to have contact and that it was Miss Graves *duty* to make this happen, otherwise she would be *failing* in her duty. But she had the *power* to put matters to right.

The poor Miss Graves did not suspect that maybe the reason for Gregory's demand to see Sam was to relish in the enjoyment of knowing that Joanne would be feeling powerless to protect her precious little son from being compelled to have contact visits.

Miss Graves arranged to interview Sam at her offices. She had a floor to herself in an office block on the other side of town.

Joanne and Sam went up in the lift to the third floor. When the lift doors opened, Joanne and Sam stepped out into a corridor lined with posters. The theme on the posters was the rights of the father to have access to the child. Joanne looked at the walls, aghast. She scanned the walls. Where were the posters about the rights of the mother? It began to dawn on Joanne that Miss Graves was now in her element. The mouse had grown fangs and claws and she exuded power and authority. What was intended to be liberation for Sam through someone representing his thoughts and wishes to the Court was obviously not going to happen. This was the nearest thing to a set-up that could be contrived.

The corridor opened out into a large room and Miss Graves's consulting room was partitioned off the main room with translucent glass-like walls and a flimsy pre-fabricated light brown door. There was only one window and that was on the back wall of her consulting room and the light was shared through the glass-like walls between the two rooms. A low long bench ran beneath the window with toys lined along it and in the middle of the room there was a small low red table and tiny chairs to match.

Miss Graves told Joanne to wait outside in the corridor and lead Sam into the room, closing the door behind her.

Joanne looked about her; there were a couple of cheap wooden chairs and some free magazines on a small table. She felt restless. Something was wrong, really wrong. Her instinct was to rush into the consulting room and rescue Sam from Miss Graves' clutches. But then what? They would all be back in Court and Miss Graves and Gregory would be able to complain that Joanne had not allowed Sam to be independently interviewed.

Joanne paced up and down the corridor. She could not sit down. She flicked through the magazines: just superficialities and nothing to distract her from the anxiety she felt for Sam.

She walked back to the glass-like partition. She could see Miss Graves at her desk on the left and the blurred outline of Sam at the far end of the room under the window, his back turned to Miss Graves as he concentrated on the cars. He was kneeling down and had positioned himself to the height of the little cars, his head on one side to study one of them as he pushed it along the bench.

Joanne crept along the side of the main room getting closer to the partition. Perhaps she would be able to hear something of what was going on. Miss Graves had her back to Joanne and was now standing next to Sam watching him play.

"Sam," said Miss Graves trying to get Sam's attention, "what do you like doing when you go to your dad's?"

Sam shrugged his shoulders, while continuing to study the wheels of the little car.

Miss Graves tried again,

"What colour is your dad's car?"

"Black," said Sam. Then he turned around to look at Miss Graves, "and its always dirty and smelly!"

"Lots of cars smell, they all have their own particular smell. Maybe it's the leather seats that smell?"

"They're not leather, they're sort of cloth. Anyway it's not the seats, its all the rotten food in the back. They throw what they don't want onto the back seats, or onto the floor. It's disgusting!"

"Well maybe your dad is too busy and hasn't time to clean it up. I bet he does it before you go and see him again."

"But he *doesn't* do it. He makes *me* do it!"

"Lots of children have the job of cleaning the car Sam!"

"Yes, but it makes me feel sick! When I picked up the bags they had dried up bits of old meat and things inside and bugs crawling all over them and the coke cans are all sticky!" Sam shuddered at the memory; he really didn't like creepy crawlies, although he knew he wasn't meant to admit it.

"I don't know why they throw the sandwiches in the back, that's wasting food. There is never any food in the *fridge*. If I go to the *fridge* to get something to eat, it's always empty, except maybe some butter and some mouldy old cheese. There's no milk or orange juice. No chocolate biscuits or crisps. I always feel *starving* there and another thing, no one seems to eat breakfast."

"Well your dad is very busy. Dads are not very good at doing the shopping and making sure there is food in the fridge, but I bet he can cook nice things."

Sam shrugged his shoulders again,

"Well his girlfriend is not bad at pasta and tomato soup. I usually go to my room to have that."

"Would you like a drink of squash and some biscuits?" Miss Graves offered as she got up and went to the windowsill where there was a jug of squash and a small tine of biscuits.

"Yes please."

Miss Graves handed Sam a glass of orange squash. He looked at the pale yellow fluid in the glass. It wasn't real orange juice and it tasted funny. It reminded him of the bath water when it came out of the tap a funny colour. Sam studied the murky looking fluid in the glass and said:

"I don't like it when he makes me share the bath with him. He says that I have to share the bath because otherwise it's a waste of water."

"Well you are his son, so that should be ok!"

"But he laughs at me. Calls me puny. I don't like it!"

"You could ask if you could get into the bath *after* him."

"He says I can't do that because the water will get cold."

"Well there *has* been a water shortage, we've had quite a drought recently and very little rain this year."

Sam pondered on this.

"But then why do I have to get undressed in front of him and his girlfriend and why do I have to share a room with them sometimes? I don't like it when they call me names and stare at me . . . and they argue all night; I can't sleep."

Sam found it not so bad telling Miss Graves. He sometimes told his mum about the things that upset him, but then *she* got upset and he didn't like to see her upset.

"I wish he wouldn't send his girlfriend to pick me up. I don't think she likes me. As soon as we get back to his house she just tells me to sit on their smelly settee and watch TV and then she disappears. Sometimes she locks me in the house while she goes out. I thought I was meant to be seeing my *dad*, not his *girlfriend*."

"Most boys would be delighted if all they were told to do was watch TV."

"Yes, but after a while it gets boring. They don't have computers or games or toys and I'm all on my own, like for *all day*."

"I'm sure his girlfriend is only helping out. If your dad is working, it's hard for him to always have time off to see you."

"But I need to do my homework and I need someone to help me with it and I can never find where they put my homework bag.

"And they keep calling me names like dyslexic and dyspraxic and say that I'm doing badly at school. I just need someone to help me! I *want* to do well, I *like* my school and I *like* my teachers, they are all *really* nice."

Sam put his head in his hands and started to rock slowly to and fro.

"Nothing makes sense," he went on, "They want me to do well at school, but don't help me to do my homework. They want me to go on visits, but when I get there they go out and leave me, or I'm just left with his girlfriend. I don't see any point in the visits, they don't really want me around anyway."

"I'm sure your dad is very fond of you. In fact, I know he is. It's just that he's not very good at looking after children."

Miss Graves started to make a few notes in the folder she held in her hand. Joanne sensed that the interview was coming to an end and quietly stepped away from the consulting room partition and pretended to be reading a poster on the wall. Miss Graves wound up the interview, she told Sam that he had no choice about the visits; that was the law. He had to visit Gregory and Gregory had the right to see him.

Miss Graves came out of her consulting room with a glum Sam behind her. Sam looked up at Joanne and rushed forward to hug her.

"How did you get on?" asked Joanne looking anxiously into Sam's little face. Of course she had heard most of what Sam had said before when he used to grumble about his visits and now that Joanne had heard Miss Graves dismissing Sam's complaints, she knew what was coming next.

Miss Graves pronounced her findings,

"Sam should go on visits to Gregory every other weekend. Fathers are not always the most organised at looking after children, but it is important that contact is made."

"But surely, if Sam is unhappy on these visits what is the point of them?"

"It wouldn't matter even if Mr Franks was in prison, the children still have to have contact with the father."

What a waste of time *that* interview was! Joanne took Sam by the hand and led him to the lift. There was no point in saying any more. It would just fall on deaf ears. Miss Graves was not there to help Sam; she was there to make sure he went on contact visits to see Gregory.

Sam's school was getting tired of all the proceedings and suggested that Joanne find him another school with more individual teaching, which could help Sam concentrate just on the major subjects such as maths and English and suggested St Luke's.

St Luke's School was just up the road from home and Sam could even walk there. The headmaster, Edward Williams was the maths teacher and his wife was the English teacher. The couple set up the school for children who were bright, but had had a poor start on the educational ladder. Either they had been unhappy at the previous school, had suffered from bullying or came from unsettled homes. The aim was to teach the essential subjects, almost on a one to one basis. There were only about eight pupils to the class and special attention was given to those who needed it.

Chris bought Sam a new bicycle so that it would make it more fun getting to school and a mobile phone to keep for emergencies.

Sam settled in well at St Luke's. All the staff were highly motivated and enthusiastic teachers who made learning fun and an adventure. Edward Williams had three children of his own and was sympathetic to Sam's predicament. He became Sam's confidante. Someone Sam could talk to about anything and everything, at any time; he was a real friend.

Sam so loved St Luke's that he would get up early and be at school by eight o'clock, even though school did not start until eight forty-five! He would help set out the desks and books. Edward would give him money to buy hot chocolate and croissants from the local shop and pupils and staff would sit together and have an extra breakfast before school started. At last Sam was happy and made a lot of friends. The staff thought he was a charming and delightful boy with a great sense of humour. Sam, at nine years old, was now getting back on track with his education.

St Luke's almost became a refuge for Sam, a place where he could pour out his troubles. He was miserable on his visits to Gregory, but at least he was able to talk it over with Edward when he got back to school.

Edward would always ask Sam how the weekend had gone, it seemed sense to let him get everything out of his system and then Sam would be better able to concentrate on his schoolwork. It was easier for Sam to talk to Edward because he would listen and sympathise and they could talk it over together, whereas his mum was more likely to become upset.

When Sam was away with Gregory, the only way Sam could keep in touch with Joanne and Chris was with his mobile 'phone. He kept it hidden at all times and slept with it under his pillow. Sometimes Sam would be away with Gregory for several days and Joanne and Chris had no idea where he was. Then they would get a phone call and they were relieved to know that at least he was all right. But contact visits remained fraught with anxiety and Joanne would get tearful 'phone calls of "Mum . . . Mum . . . I miss you . . ." and Sam would sob down the 'phone.

Sometimes Sam would be away several days and when he 'phoned Joanne, she would try to sound cheery,

"Sam! Hey Sam, how are you doing? Where are you?"

This time he replied,

"I don't know . . . somewhere in France . . . I've been trying to ring you, but I couldn't get through . . . then this kind lady told me how to put the numbers in for England. Mum . . . Mum . . . I miss you, I feel so sad . . . I miss Alex . . . I miss Chris . . . I want to come home, please, please help me," his voice broke into sobs.

"Where's Gregory? How could you get to France without a passport?" Joanne asked

"He made me hide in the car with jackets and things on top of me . . . Mum I want to come home . . ."

Joanne could picture it all, Gregory driving up to passport control, the car piled untidily with jackets, case books etc and when Gregory was asked if he was travelling alone, Gregory would of course answer "Yes!" and then "No" to the question of have you got any pets or anyone else accompanying you. It couldn't have been easier!

"Mum . . . I got to go now, I can see him coming . . . I love you . . . I'll call you again later . . . bye," and the 'phone went dead.

At least Sam had the sense to 'phone and keep in touch.

It was a few weeks later when Sam was on another visit that Joanne and Chris got a 'phone call late Sunday night just as they were going to bed.

"Where are you this time?" asked Joanne

"I don't know, somewhere near the sea . . . I'm in a hotel . . . Gregory's at a wedding or something . . . and I'm locked in the hotel room . . . at least there's a TV . . . but I'm bored . . . I've been here for hours . . . Mum I want to come home . . . I don't see the point of going on visits when all I do is sit in a hotel room all day . . . and I'm starving . . ."

The next Friday visit, Sam had only been gone a few hours, when the 'phone rang.

Joanne could hear sobbing and knew that it was Sam.

"Where are you my little guy?" she asked

"Mum . . . Mum . . . I'm at Gregory's . . . I've had it . . . I can't take any more of this . . . you got to get me home . . . out of this mess . . ."

"Where's Gregory?"

"I don't know . . . downstairs somewhere . . ." Sam started to calm down a bit at hearing Joanne's voice and continued "I locked myself in the bedroom so they couldn't get at me."

"Who are you talking about?"

"Gregory and that mad girl friend of his, Elaine . . . she's so mean . . . she's mean *all* the time . . . so I came upstairs and locked myself in the bedroom . . . they don't want me to call you, so I'm trying to speak quietly . . . they won't let me 'phone you . . . they don't want me to use the ordinary 'phone . . . they don't know I've got the mobile . . . but I have to be quiet or they'll get really mad at me . . ."

There was a pause and then, Sam whispered,

"She's coming . . . I can hear her . . . I got to go now . . ." and Joanne could hear someone shouting Sam's name in the background just as he switched the 'phone off.

Joanne could not sleep. She lay awake, lying next to Chris, so that her body touched his. She loved to feel the warmth of him, it was comforting and she lay listening to his breathing. She knew he was not sleeping either, but what was there to say? It was difficult to know what to do.

Just after midnight Joanne got another call from Sam,

"Mum . . . Mum . . ." came the sobs, "I can't sleep . . . I want to come home . . . I hate it here . . . Elaine keeps shouting at me to let her in . . . but I won't . . . I don't see why I should . . . she's mean . . . she's horrible . . . I hate her . . . she'll hit me if I let her in . . . you got to get me out of here . . ." then Sam's 'phone went dead.

Joanne wasn't sure whether Sam had switched off the 'phone or whether the battery had run out. She lay there in the dark, trying to picture all that was going on.

Chris suggested that in the morning they should go round to Gregory's house and make sure that Sam was all right. Joanne switched on the bedside light so that she could see to text Sam a message. If Sam's 'phone was still working, he would feel that they were keeping in touch with him.

"*Dearest Sam, call me in the morning if you can and if things are not good we'll come and collect you. We love you so much. Love Mum xxxx*"

Joanne did not hear any more from Sam until they were finishing breakfast,

"Mum . . . Mum . . . it's me, Sam . . ."

"Where are you?"

"I'm in the kitchen . . . I'm using their 'phone. Everybody's still upstairs in bed. I think . . . my 'phone's run out of battery . . . please Mum, please come and get me I hate it here . . ."

Then Joanne heard loud footsteps as though someone was striding into the room.

Then a man's voice shouted,

"What are you doing? Put that 'phone down! I thought I'd find you in here . . ." and the 'phone went dead.

Joanne decided to call the police and see if they had a view on the situation.

The PC at the other end of the 'phone took down the details, names and addresses and so on and then she asked,

"Have you reason to believe that the child is in danger or is being hurt in any way?" Joanne could only describe the 'phone calls that she had had from Sam and the fact that Gregory had a history of violence, but she said that as far as Sam was concerned, it was possibly more verbal abuse than physical and the fact that Sam was being kept against his will.

The PC gave Joanne the incident number as a reference and said that she would put a call through to the local station and have someone call on Gregory to see if the child was all right.

Joanne asked their neighbour Michael and Brenda to look after Alex while Joanne and Chris got into the car and drove to Gregory's house. They parked a little way down the street so they could observe what went on.

After waiting about fifteen minutes a police car arrived with two police officers and they too parked a little way from the house. One of them got out of the police car and walked to the front door and rang the bell. No one came to the door and after several more rings, the police officer returned to his car and spoke to his female colleague. After a while he pulled out a radio and made a call back to the police station.

Then Joanne caught sight of Sam on her left, coming across the road. Gregory had Sam's arm gripped high above the elbow and was frog marching him back to the house.

Gregory saw the police car. He seemed annoyed and increased his pace, pulling Sam along with him.

The male police officer got out of the police car and briskly walked towards Gregory's driveway. Joanne could just hear the police officer's voice as he called out,

"Excuse me Sir . . ." but Gregory ignored the police officer, turning his head away from him as though he hadn't heard and hurried on. The police officer increased his stride and got to the driveway first, preventing Gregory from going any further. Then the lady officer got out of the car and walked over to Sam. She squatted down next to him and spoke to him, while her colleague talked to Gregory. Gregory gesticulated with his free arm as though he was very angry, but Joanne couldn't hear what he was saying.

After a while Gregory was allowed to go on up the driveway to his front door, still holding onto Sam's arm, he unlocked his front door and pushed Sam into the house.

The police officer then went back to his car to report back to the station, while the lady officer came over to Joanne and Chris's car. Joanne got out of the car to meet her.

"Well", she said, "I presume you are Mrs Parry, the mother?" Joanne nodded, "Your son does not seem to be hurt and he says he will be coming home tomorrow . . . I can see that there is tension between the two, but if he says that he is not hurt then there is not much we can do. I suggest you talk to your solicitor and try to make a more acceptable arrangement."

Joanne thanked the lady officer. Well, there wasn't much more they could do. Sam was too little to stand up to Gregory. He would not have been able to tell the officer why he was unhappy. At least not with Gregory standing over him, gripping his arm and no doubt squeezing it hard to remind Sam that he should do as he was told.

Chris drove Joanne back home.

"It's amazing," exclaimed Joanne, "that Gregory can treat Sam in this way . . ."

Chris just looked at her and shook his head. They would have to wait for tomorrow before they would have Sam back home with them.

Sunday evening arrived at last. This time Sam was dropped back home soon after six and there was enough time for Sam and Alex to have some supper together and have a play before bedtime. Soon everyone was tucked up in bed and asleep.

φ

It was about one in the morning when Joanne was woken by the sound of sobbing and she made her way to Sam's room and found him sitting bolt upright in bed, with his eyes wide open, but apparently not seeing anything and shouting between uncontrolled sobs. Joanne sat next to him, stroking his back. She couldn't hold him, he was too rigid. Tears stung her eyes as she felt his agony and frustration.

Eventually Sam relaxed enough for her to hold him and rock him in her arms. As she rocked him she noticed a note lying on the floor next to the bed. It was Sam's writing. She bent down and picked it up. It read:

"In the real world it's the bad guy's that win, not the good guys. It's not like the movies when the good guys win. In the real world it's the bad guys that win."

It was scrawled in red crayon and he had drawn a circle with a sad face at the bottom of the note, like the teachers did in schoolbooks if the work was not good. Joanne looked closer at the drawing, it had tears coming from the eyes, Joanne felt sick in her stomach, this was all too much. This was the sort of thing that the Courts should take notice of, but she knew that if she sent this to the Judge, he would simply say that she had told Sam what to write and that it was not Sam's words.

The next day was Monday and Joanne decided to report the weekend incident to the local child protection team, to see if they could help. They asked Joanne to bring Sam in to interview him and having dropped off Alex at his new primary school, Joanne drove Sam down to their offices.

The child protection team were in plain clothes so as to appear casual and non-threatening to the children. They explained to Joanne that there were three rooms, one where a lady officer would chat to Sam while he played with toys and she would ask him questions. There were cameras and video links from that room to the room next door where an officer monitored the video and cameras and made copies for police records. The third room was for Joanne to sit and wait their findings.

Sam was taken to the playroom and the lady officer sat on the settee chatting to him as he amused himself with some toys they had laid out for him, while Joanne was led to the waiting room and given a cup of tea.

It seemed like an age to Joanne before the officer finally entered the room and sat down next to Joanne. She looked sympathetically at Joanne and Joanne knew by her consoling manner what was coming next.

"Well!" the officer said, "Yes it's bad; but not *bad enough* to relieve Sam from his obligation to have contact."

The officer could see the distress in Joanne's face. She continued:

"If it helps . . . I asked Sam to give me a score out of ten for all of you. For Gregory he gave one out of ten, for you he gave nine out of ten and for Chris he gave twenty!"

The officer apologised again; she said that although she had no doubt that in Joanne's opinion, Gregory was ill-treating Sam, it wasn't *bad enough* to take any action.

Once again, Joanne felt let down. How *bad* did it have to be?

Chapter Nine

Achilles Heel?

Gregory's girl friend Elaine was certainly not pleased at having to share her weekends with Sam and she was determined to get rid of him, somehow.

She had rummaged through Gregory's filing cabinet and discovered the 1989 papers on the IVF clinic. Maybe that was why Sam looked so different to Gregory. They did not seem to share any resemblance to each other, either in looks or character. Maybe, just maybe, Sam was not his child.

Elaine knew that somehow she needed to get a DNA test done. It was fairly simple to get hair or saliva from Gregory, but not so easy from Sam. Or was it?

Elaine always made Sam stay in his room until she allowed him to come to the kitchen to eat. She made it very clear that he was not welcome and when he was allowed into the kitchen to eat, she would make snide remarks under her breath, trying to make him as unhappy as she possibly could.

Elaine called Sam to come to the kitchen and told him to sit at the table out of her way. Sam dutifully sat down with his back to Elaine, trying to ignore the incessant criticisms being thrown at him. He looked out of the window trying to block out the noise. Elaine could certainly rattle on and Sam wasn't concentrating when Elaine put the bowl of pasta in front of him. He looked down at the bowl and put his hand out to reach for a fork but his arm caught the edge of the bowl and the mixture of pasta and tomato soup went hurling across the wooden floor. That was the moment Elaine had been waiting for, she grabbed Sam's hair and used it to shake his head, she hit him with a saucepan that she in her hand and thumped him so hard on his back he coughed up the chewing gum he had been secretly eating.

That was all Elaine needed. Some strands of Sam's hair and saliva and some samples from Gregory.

She carefully put them in separate sample containers to take them to the local clinic that did DNA tests.

φ

Some weeks later, Joanne picked up the post off the doormat and saw there was an envelope addressed to her. She didn't recognise the blue handwriting and curiously opened the envelope. Inside was a photocopy of a DNA report. Reading down the document, she saw that it was duly stamped and dated and stated that according to the DNA tests carried out at the clinic,

Re. putative father: Gregory Franks: paternity excluded.

Gregory was not Sam's father!

Joanne was over-joyed; now, surely now, Gregory could not insist that Sam visit him.

Elaine told Gregory about the DNA results and he was not pleased. Elaine was disappointed. She had hoped that he would forget Sam and concentrate on a relationship with her.

At the next Court hearing, Judge Sissens was furious, outraged that such a test had been performed without the express permission from the Court. He fumed and spluttered. His face was livid with rage. Gregory swore that it made no difference to his feelings for Sam and Judge Sissens insisted that Sam should continue to have contact with Mr Gregory Franks, regardless of whether or not the DNA test proved Gregory to be the father.

Gregory was now even more determined to be as difficult as he possible could. He started to take Sam out of St Luke's on Friday lunchtimes, purportedly for lunch, but he used the excuse to set off early with Sam to his house in the country and avoid the Friday night traffic. St Luke's reported that Sam's homework was not being done and Joanne got the feeling that once again the school was becoming impatient with the disruption.

Gregory was irritated that Edward Williams was not sympathetic to Gregory's need to set off early on a Friday. In turn he criticised the school and complained that Sam was not achieving a high enough standard and threatened to sue the school for failing Sam in his education.

Gregory then insisted on having Sam assessed. He was determined to have Sam declared dyslexic and should go to a special needs school, rather than admitting that it could be the emotional disturbance and the lack of completing his schoolwork that was causing Sam to fall behind.

All in all, six independent educational consultants assessed Sam. Every time Gregory got a report that said Sam was a perfectly normal little boy with perfectly normal IQ scores, he insisted on having another assessment done.

In November 2001 Edward Williams sent Joanne a copy of a letter he had received from Gregory. Gregory had organised yet another assessment, this time by Harley House, a remedial School. Edward scribbled on a complements slip to Joanne that he did not think Sam would need the resources of a remedial school, but if that is what Gregory wanted, then he should oblige.

What was Gregory up to now? Sam didn't need the help of a remedial school. Joanne 'phoned Edward at lunch time and found him free for a few minutes between classes,

"Well," pondered Edward, "we do need to think about the next school, but it's a bit early yet for Sam to do entry exams. Sam is eleven and I think he would find the transition to the next school easier at twelve or thirteen. Porter House School is a school that would suit Sam. It's in town, but has access to local playing fields. It has a reputation for being a caring school; they put pupils in three grades A, B and C and the school would take Sam through his GCSE and A levels. I know the headmaster well and could drop him a line if you like? I suggest you look at the school in February or March next year with a view to entry in September 2003."

φ

In March 2002 Joanne received a letter from Mr Rafter, the headmaster of Porter House School, inviting Sam to come for an interview with his parents.

Joanne, Chris and Sam stood at the entrance to Porter House School. The tall black decorative wrought iron gates gave an imposing feel to the building and when Joanne pressed the entry bell the gates automatically started to open. Mr Rafter's secretary greeted them at the front door and showed them into the waiting room that originally must have been the old dining room.

Porter House School seemed ideal for Sam, it had a friendly atmosphere, a large Victorian town house, three stories high with a walled back garden that had been turned into a playground and it was only a short bike ride from home.

They had only been there a few moments when Mr Rafter appeared at the door beaming a welcoming smile and held out his hand to shake Sam's hand.

"This must be Sam!" he said: "You look a fine young man! I understand that you have some of your schoolwork to show me? Let's all go upstairs to my office where it will be a bit quieter, all the pupils will be pouring out of class for lunch break soon! They can make quite a racket you know," he said with a grin.

Mr Rafter led the way up the wide mahogany staircase to his office on the first floor. He seated himself behind his large mahogany desk, with his computer and piles of schoolbooks and told them to take a seat. He looked as though he was in his forties, with shiny black hair and his bright yellow jumper made him seem a very jolly sort of fellow. He lent over his desk towards Sam.

"Now Sam! Do show me what you've got in that bag of yours!" he said encouragingly, as he fiddled with his 'Garfield' mug with pens and pencils rattling inside.

Sam took out his Maths and English books and gave them to Mr Rafter.

"I like history and drawing, so I brought those too," said Sam proudly, "*and* some of my war hammer models!"

Mr Rafter was impressed with Sam's neatly laid out work and admired his models, which he knew must have taken many hours of patient work. He suggested to Joanne and Chris that Sam should attend a day in class to see how he got on with the other pupils. His secretary would write and suggest which day Sam should attend and he would also write to Edward Williams and let him know the plan.

Before they left, Mr Rafter gave them a little tour of the school. It had many winding staircases leading from one floor to the next and lots of informal classrooms of various sizes. The basement had been turned into washrooms and cloakrooms full of lockers and benches and at the far end was the school canteen. As pupils approached the canteen, they stopped to exchange a few words with Mr Rafter. Sam thought he was very friendly, a bit like Edward Williams and it made him feel quite at ease.

The following week Joanne received a letter inviting Sam to attend Porter House School for the day. He was to spend a full day and join in everything that the other pupils did. He needed to bring only a pencil case for class and tracksuit and trainers for games.

Sam found all the boys and girls very friendly and helpful. The school felt just like someone's large house, he liked the teachers and the food wasn't bad either.

Mr Rafter was pleased that Sam had got on well with the other pupils and had produced some good work in class. He wrote to Joanne offering Sam a place at the school,

"I am delighted to be able to offer Sam a place in Year 9 for entry in September 2003. A place may become available before this time in Year 8, in which case I will contact you. I would ask that Sam sit a setting examination prior to joining us in September 2003 (for grading into classes A, B or C) or earlier if applicable.

Yours sincerely,"

Joanne was both relieved and delighted. She knew Sam tended to be nervous and panic when being tested, but he could apply himself with confidence in the more relaxed atmosphere of being part of a class.

It was about a month later when Joanne found a long roll of faxed letters waiting for her in the study. She looked at the pile and dreaded what it might contain. She sighed resignedly as she sifted through the mound of paper. They were copies of correspondence between Gregory, Harley House School, St Luke's and Porter House School and she carefully put them in date order to try and make sense of them.

The first was Harley House's assessment of Sam. The report stated that Sam's reading age was nine years and was well behind the standard needed for an eleven year old and that his score in his maths exam had been thirty out of a hundred.

Next there was a letter from Edward Williams saying that he did not agree with the scores in the assessment.

So far, so good, thought Joanne. Then she picked up the next letter that was from Gregory to Mr Rafter,

"Thank you for your school brochure. I spoke to your admissions secretary yesterday about Sam. It was a surprise to me that Sam had been for an interview, although I knew Mr and Mrs Parry intended to visit. I attach the assessment from Harley House School. I know Mr Williams is hopeful that he can improve Sam's performance so that he can pass the required setting exam for entry in September 2003.

I would hope to be allowed to visit Porter House, if it felt that the school could cater for Sam's needs. The present problem is that he is up to 3 years behind his chronological age, the 'lag' having increased since he has been at St Luke's.

Sam has been diagnosed as suffering from dyslexia and visual auditory processing problems and Harley House confirm this in their assessment of Sam.

I hope you are now in a position to advise.

Yours sincerely,"

The next was Mr Rafter's reply to Gregory,

"You and I have had a number of conversations about Sam over the last few weeks and I would like to express my concerns.

When Sam came to the school and joined in the classes I was very impressed with him and convinced that he will be ready for us

in September 2003, Year 9. This is now contradicted by Harley House's assessment of Sam that you sent me.

Sam will need to sit a setting exam to enable us to place him in the correct English and Mathematics groups. If he falls below our lowest set, it will not be in Sam's interest for him to join us.

I have every confidence that this will not happen and that he will produce work up to, at least, the lowest set.

I understand that you wish Sam to attend Harley House for remedial help and that Mrs Parry wishes Sam to remain at St Luke's and have extra tuition there.

I do hope that matters can soon be resolved between you.

Yours sincerely."

What on earth made Gregory do such a thing? How could he ruin Sam's chance of a going to such a good school? What was he doing, putting doubt in Mr Rafter's mind, when Mr Rafter had been so impressed with Sam?

In April Joanne received another demand to appear in Court, now the sixty-third hearing. Gregory had made an application to the Court to review Sam's education.

Joanne braced herself. What had Gregory in mind now?

Gregory knew that Joanne and Chris had not much money to spend on these cases; maybe he was just trying to run them dry.

ф

Joanne sat at a table outside the Court doors, a coffee in her hands. There were several other people also waiting for their cases to be called. The list was posted outside the Court door, the cases would be called in order, but you never knew how long each case would be. She saw the name of the Judge who would be hearing the cases today, but it didn't mean anything to her, she had not heard of this Judge before.

A clerk with a black flowing robe over a dark suit approached Joanne. She checked that Joanne's name was on the list and informed her that she should wait outside the Court until her case was called, according to the list for the day and the ushers would then conduct her into Court. Joanne's was the first case on the list, Court opened at ten thirty, it was now ten; another thirty minutes and they would be in Court.

Joanne's attention was drawn toward the sound of loud footsteps and jovial voices. Looking up she saw Gregory with one of the Judges chatting away as old friends, his pompous voice could be heard echoing down the corridor, interspersed with loud guffaws.

Both men strode along, their suits straining to cover their large bellies. Gregory was in his element, obviously on first name terms and very at home with the Judge.

"James!" Gregory was laughing, "and did you hear about Henry's disastrous holiday?"

It sounded like they were old drinking mates; well maybe they were.

Seeing Joanne, Gregory turned his back to her. He leaned towards the Judge and they resumed their conversation in more hushed tones.

Joanne pretended not to notice. She occupied herself sipping her coffee and hoped that she looked calm and unruffled. The sun was shining through the window onto the table where she sat and she decided to take a walk outside on the paved courtyard.

As the doors swung open, she felt the warm sun on her face. It was refreshing to be outside and she slowly walked up and down the path. She tried to clear her head and make sense of all that had happened.

Gregory was difficult to weigh up. He needed to feel in charge; he liked to be feared. He also enjoyed the thrill of inflicting pain both mentally and physically. Maybe Patrick was right, Gregory had been dealing with villains too long and some of their life style had rubbed off on him.

Joanne slowly made her way back across the courtyard to the Courts. It was ten twenty and not long before Court was to begin. She did not want to be late so she walked back to her seat outside the Courtroom door and looked around to see if she could see Gregory. He was nowhere to be seen. She was expecting to see him striding up and down the corridor as if he owned the place, trying to intimidate and appear in complete control of the situation. But where was he this time? Maybe he had disappeared to get a coffee.

A few more minutes passed and Joanne was drawn by the sound of the Court doors swinging open. Gregory came striding out!

Joanne could not believe it. What was he doing in Court even before the Courts had officially opened? Joanne felt her stomach tense up in knots. What was he up to now? He hadn't given her any papers this time, so what was his plan?

The usher stood outside the Court doors and shouted,

"Case of Parry and Franks!"

There were two doors that led into the Court, one on the far right, one of the far left. Joanne was led into the Court by the right door and Gregory entered by the left. Joanne took her seat.

"Court rise!" announced the clerk and in came the Judge in his robes.

Everyone bowed to the Judge and then the Judge sat down, followed by everyone else. Once seated, Joanne anxiously looked up to see who the Judge was today. Under the wig, Joanne could see that it was the Judge that Gregory had been chatting to outside Court! Once again Gregory had the upper hand and she felt trapped.

Gregory stood up first and opened the hearing by announcing that he was making this application to put Sam into a special needs school. He told the Court that Sam was not achieving at St Luke's and that Sam would receive a much better education at Harley House School.

Gregory was speaking to the Judge as though it was a foregone conclusion and this was only a formality that he appeared today.

Joanne stood up to protest.

Judge Gibbons looked up at her and frowned,

"You will have your say shortly," he commanded.

Gregory continued,

"Sam is no longer a pupil at St Luke's and I have made provision for him to go to Harley House School this September, the school has assessed him and has offered him a place.

Joanne could not believe what she was hearing. How could it be that Sam was no longer at St Luke's, he had gone to school as usual this morning.

Sam loved being at St Luke's; it was like a second home to him. It was unheard of to *contemplate* moving Sam at this stage.

Joanne started to panic inside, she felt choked, what was going on? What had Gregory done? How could Gregory do this? What was he talking about? How can he just take over like this? It would break Sam's heart to leave St. Luke's, it's too soon. Sam still had at least another year to run at St Luke's. He was only eleven. He wasn't due to leave St Luke's for another year or two.

Joanne stood up,

"Please, please I beg you, I don't know anything about this. Mr Franks has no right to make decisions without me. Please allow me to call the headmaster of St Luke's, Mr Williams and ask him to come to Court. Sam is happy at St Luke's and he's doing fine! Mr Franks can't take Sam out of school just like that! Or *you* could call him," she added desperately, "and speak to him yourself. I can give you the number to call."

Judge Gibbons considered what to do.

"I suggest that you go outside the Courtroom Mrs Parry. I will give you twenty minutes to make a call to Mr Williams and then I want you to come back and report to me."

Outside the Courtroom Joanne dialled the number for St Luke's, her heart pounding, Edward came to the 'phone, Joanne couldn't stop the tears streaming down her face.

"Please, please Edward . . . tell me what's going on . . . what on earth has Gregory done . . . ?"

Edward explained that over the last couple of terms Gregory had made life unbearably fraught, with threats of suing the school as Sam was not achieving as high a standard as he believed Sam should achieve. Gregory had sent long complicated letters full of legal jargon giving grounds for suing the school and had 'phoned several times a day demanding to speak to Edward, taking him away from the lessons that he was teaching. He had called at the school, demanding to see Edward and other members of staff. It was simply impossible for Edward and the rest of the staff to continue to educate Sam.

Edward said how fond he was of Sam, but Gregory had terminated the contract with the school. There was no provision for Sam to go back there next term.

Joanne pleaded with Edward to take Sam back, but he said that he couldn't, he was sorry, but he really couldn't. Gregory had just made it impossible to have Sam at the school. The only way Edward could see his way of having Sam back, was if the Court could offer him protection from Gregory interfering with Sam's education and be prevented from contacting the school. Edward said that Joanne's solicitor, Elizabeth, had done her best to try to secure some sort of protection against Gregory, but it seemed not that easy to organise. Edward said he would visit Sam over the holidays, have a chat with him, take him some schoolbooks and give him some work to do.

Back in Court Judge Gibbons demanded,

"Well Mrs Parry, what did Edward Williams have to say to you?"

"He said Sam didn't have a place at St Luke's for next term. But that's all because Mr Franks here took Sam out . . ."

"That's not the point!" bellowed Judge Gibbons, "Does Sam have a place at St Luke's next term . . . or not?"

Joanne protested again,

"Mr Franks took Sam . . ."

"Mrs Parry! Answer the question! Does Sam have a place at St Luke's or not. *Yes* or *no!*"

Joanne opened her mouth to speak.

"Simply, *yes* or *no* Mrs Parry!" demanded Judge Gibbons.

Joanne could feel tears of frustration welling up. This was silly, she mustn't be defeated, she mustn't let Gregory Franks see that she was upset; he would *so* love to see her suffer.

Finally with head bowed, she said,

"No."

"I see!" scoffed Judge Gibbons; "Sam has no place at St. Luke's. The law states that every child is to attend school."

Gregory stood up and addressed Judge Gibbons in his usual pompous way:

"My Lord! May I interject? I would suggest that if Mrs Parry is against sending Sam to a special needs school, then Sam should attend the local state school."

What a turn around! First it's one school then it's the next! He just doesn't care. Anger and frustration was building up inside her.

"Sam doesn't have a place a St Luke's because *you* took him out of his school, the school he loved. *You* left Sam with no school to go to . . ."

What was this man doing? Why was Judge Gibbons not doing anything about it? Judge Gibbons could order St Luke's to take Sam back: the Courts had that authority.

Judge Gibbons' voice boomed out:

"Then it's agreed!"

"No, its *not* agreed," protested Joanne.

"It *is* agreed Mrs Parry, I heard you say so!"

"I did *not* agree," persisted Joanne. "Sam is not even Mr Frank's son, Gregory Franks is not the father and he has no right to do this . . ."

"You're behaviour, Mrs Parry, is outrageous, I will hear no more. You did agree. It is now in the Court records and I will not hear any more on the matter!"

Judge Gibbons stood up and left the Court.

Gutted. There wasn't another word for it. Joanne felt as though someone had drained the last bit of life out of her.

What was she going to say to Sam? How could she break the news to him?

On the way home, sitting back in the taxi, Joanne swore to herself that she was not going to be beaten; this man was not going to ruin Sam's life.

She had to find someone who would be prepared to go out on a limb; to do something out of the ordinary; someone who was not frightened of the Judge's disapproval.

Why was everyone so frightened of the Judge?

Joanne was fed up of hearing what the Judge *would* or *would not* like. What he *would* allow and what he *would not*.

For weeks Sam cried and cried. He couldn't understand why he couldn't go back to his beloved St Luke's. Sam's friends called to see him throughout the summer holidays, but it still didn't ease the pain, they were there and he was nowhere.

Edward Williams kept in constant touch with Sam inviting him to join in activities happening at St Luke's and remained Sam's confidante. Edward and the other staff did their best to provide Sam with textbooks and work to do over the holidays and during the beginning of the September term, as Sam still had no school to go to.

All the local State schools were full and Joanne was left to find somewhere for Sam to go to, all the while receiving threatening calls from Gregory, saying that he would prosecute her for failing to send Sam to school.

Joanne asked Sam what he thought about Harley House School when he went for his assessment there, but Sam was quite adamant that he would not be happy there.

"I don't want to be unkind mum," Sam explained, "but I felt out of place, I didn't fit in. There were boys in wheelchairs and dribbling all the time and some of the girls couldn't talk properly and I couldn't understand what they were trying to say and it made me feel awkward, I can't really explain. You see, I don't need someone to feed me or take me to the toilet, I don't think I would fit in."

So Joanne continued to 'phone all the schools in the area, but no one had any vacancies.

Finally, Joanne received a call back from the headmistress of the International School who said that maybe she could take Sam in, depending on his standard of work. A girl had left at half term to go back to her native China because her mother was seriously ill and now there was potentially a vacancy.

Joanne duly took round some of Sam's schoolwork for the headmistress to inspect. She was happy with the neatly presented work and, after interviewing Sam, she offered him a place, even though it was half way through the term. The school seemed very caring and many of the pupils were away from their families and staying with guardians, so the atmosphere was sympathetic. Joanne was so relieved, although it meant a bus ride to get to school at least it was a school that from the start was helpful and supportive.

At the end of October the Court conceded that it was best for Sam to remain for the time being at the

International School. By now, Sam at eleven years old, was on his fourth school and the Court advised that he should not be moved again.

However, Gregory was determined to remove Sam from the International School. He had now made so many applications to the Courts that Joanne had lost count. He never informed Joanne, he just went along to Court with his Miss Graves and Joanne would only get to know when she received her copy of the latest Court Order sent to her by the Court Services.

Joanne got used to seeing the post on the doormat and the familiar brown envelopes with the Court stamp on them. She opened the latest envelope from the Court Service. Inside was a copy of yet another Court order with a compliments slip attached. The clerk had written a note to Joanne,

"This is Court Order number 72. I counted them! Kind regards."

This time Gregory had applied for contact with Sam *that weekend* and there was a penal notice attached.

"A penal notice," explained Elizabeth, "Means that you have to take it seriously Joanne! If you do not obey the Court Order you will be threatened with imprisonment. No kidding. It's for real! There is nothing Gregory would like more, than to see you sent to prison. He'd love it!"

Joanne remembered how Gregory had often described the horrors of women's prisons and she shuddered at the memory.

"Well I am *not* going to take Sam to Gregory's," said Joanne stubbornly, *"no way!"*

Elizabeth paused to consider if there was a possible way around the Court Order; a compromise for Joanne;

"Well, you *could* take Sam to Gregory's place of work; and I could inform Gregory by fax that that is where he can collect him?"

When Sam heard about the weekend visit he absolutely refused to go, but Joanne explained that Gregory would apply to have her sent to prison if she did not take Sam personally. Joanne also knew that Gregory would gladly deny that any visit had taken place; so Elizabeth's idea of taking Sam to his chambers seemed the best way to prove that the visit had taken place, so that Joanne had at least had done her part.

Joanne took Sam by taxi to Gregory's chambers.

Standing outside the old black door to Gregory's chambers Joanne studied the two black boards, one either side of the door, where the names of the members of chambers were listed in gold handwriting. Joanne opened the door and walked up the old stone steps, Sam dutifully following her behind. She looked up the staircase, it wound round and round, up and up and at each level there was an inner door to that level. The first door she came to was painted cream with big black handwriting on it saying 'Clerk'. Joanne pushed on the door; it opened easily onto a carpeted hallway with various doors leading off. As Joanne and Sam entered the hallway one of the doors opened and out stepped a clerk dressed in a dark pin stripped suit.

"Can I help you?" he enquired a little puzzled, looking from Joanne to Sam.

Joanne introduced herself. She explained why she was there with Sam. The clerk looked slightly embarrassed and went down the corridor to find the head of chambers.

The head of chambers came out of one of the rooms at the end of the corridor and walked towards Joanne and Sam. He was a tall slim gentleman, probably in his fifties with fair greying hair. He too wore a dark pin striped suit and had an air of authority about him.

"How can I be of help?" he enquired kindly.

Joanne explained that she needed him to witness the fact that she had brought Sam to Gregory's chambers and asked if he would be good enough to put it in writing on one of chamber's compliments slips, that she, Joanne, had delivered Sam for the purpose of Gregory having contact with Sam and asked him to sign and date it.

The man looked sympathetically at Joanne; of course he knew all about the proceedings, after all it had gone on for years. He duly gave Joanne a compliments slip with the statement she required.

"Come along then young man, follow me!"

Joanne kissed Sam goodbye, her eyes full of tears. Sam knew how much this was killing her inside. He gave her a hug and watched her until she disappeared through the door to go back home.

The next Court order that arrived on the doormat was Gregory's application to remove Sam from the International School and send Sam to boarding school. Gregory believed that Sam should be as far away from his mother as possible. He believed that Joanne was turning the child against him and Miss Graves supported his application.

No way! Thought Joanne and she kept wracking her brains for a way to counter Gregory's latest machination. Then she had an idea. What about the well-known Mrs Leslie Martins? Joanne had heard people talk about her; she was a child clinical psychologist who believed that the child's welfare comes first. Joanne thought it would be useless writing a letter, it would probably get lost in the bowels of the hospital post room. Instead she found the 'phone number and left a message briefly describing Sam's predicament and pleaded for Mrs Martins to see Sam.

Mrs Martins responded promptly. She said that she was fully booked. However, she had a patient coming from Greece for an appointment in three days time and if they did not confirm the booking, she could see Sam instead; so long as Joanne did not mind only having a day's notice to bring Sam along.

Joanne was delighted. She felt confident that she would really *listen* to Sam.

Two days later Joanne received a message from Mrs Martins' secretary. The Greek couple would prefer to have an appointment later in the year and Mrs Martins would be happy to see Sam in their place.

The hospital waiting room was more comfortable and welcoming than most. Joanne supposed this was because it was the private wing. A soft blue carpeted floor, with light wood tables and chairs for people to sit and read magazines while waiting to be seen.

Joanne and Chris were about to sit down with Sam when Mrs Martins walked into the room. At least Joanne presumed it was Mrs Martins; she had not met the lady before, she had only heard of her fine reputation. Mrs Martins was difficult to age, but maybe she looked older than she really was. Dressed in a smart light blue suit, she walked with a slight limp and seemed in some discomfort from her left leg, her short dark wavy hair was greying and she wore what looked like reading glasses a little way down her nose. Her face lit up as she greeted Joanne with her warm friendly smile that immediately made Joanne feel at ease.

"Mr and Mrs Parry I presume?" Then looking at Sam, "And this is Sam? How nice to meet you all!" she said enthusiastically and shook everyone's hand in turn. Then she spoke to Joanne and explained:

"The way I work is that I want you and Chris to come into my consulting room and have a chat with me. Meanwhile . . ."

Mrs Martins then bent down to Sam,

" . . . meanwhile, I want to ask Sam if he would be kind enough to wait in this nice waiting room. There are drinks in the glass cabinet," she said and motioned to a tall glass fronted cabinet with cartons of fruit juices, "and biscuits on the tables so just help yourself to anything you like." Then Mrs Martins handed a pad of lined paper and a pencil to Sam.

"Sam!" she said eagerly, "while you are waiting for us, please would you be kind enough to write me a little something about yourself. I want you to call it: 'About me'."

Sam looked up at her slightly puzzled,

"What do I write?"

"Anything. Anything you like. I just want a little essay about you. Whatever comes into your head. We will only be a few minutes, don't worry."

Sam took the pad and pencil from Mrs Martins' hand and went to the nearest table to the drinks cabinet and sat down. He watched Joanne and Chris follow Mrs. Martins into her consulting room and the door shut behind them. Sam decided he would help himself to a carton of orange juice and a chocolate biscuit and then he got to work on his essay.

Sam wrote:

"My name is Sam and I have a brother who is going to school and has been for some time and has two guinea pigs called Ginger and Spice. I am twelve and a half and I have a dog called Springer who I am very fond of and love very much as well as my family. I am very upset because Mr Franks wants to take me out of the International School that I like very much. He has already taken me out of St Luke's School, which I have not got over yet. St Luke's was the best school I would ever have gone to now and now, like losing someone really important and you really love, is lost forever and I can't stop thinking about the good old days of being there with my friends. I still remember the day when I could not go back and crying, saying to myself I am losing it. Edward was someone I liked very much and he was the head of the school. Now I am at IS school and I like it very much, but still Mr Franks wants to take me out and I just can't stand it. At this point in my life I just want to jump off a cliff because my life is dead and upsetting. It may sound stupid but that is how I feel, unless people like Mr Franks leave me to get on with my life.

If I had one wish, just one wish, it would be to stop Mr Franks messing up my life. People like Mr Franks need to leave me to get on with my life and be happy."

About twenty minutes later Mrs Martins came out of her consulting room and called over to Sam,

"Sam? Have you finished what you want to write about, or do you want some more time?"

"No, I think I've written all I want to write."

"Ok then, now why don't you swop places with your mum and Chris and come and have a chat with me in my room."

Sam dutifully followed Mrs Martins into her room while Joanne and Chris got themselves a coffee from the vending machine.

Sam liked Mrs Martins, she seemed kind and he felt comfortable talking to her, he felt she was a bit like a nice granny, he confided:

"I want to be at home where I have friends, I don't want to go to boarding school. I can't concentrate on my life and people aren't taking in what I say and the Court people do not *listen*, they just feel I should be told what to do as if I have no part in it. I just want to be with my family and be happy and have a nice life. All this has ruined my childhood. They must give my life back to me."

Mrs Martins then went on to formally assess Sam, to record his current IQ scores and make a full and proper report.

A copy of Sam's writings and a transcription of what he had confided to Mrs Martins was sent to Joanne and Chris along with her report.

Mrs Martins wrote,

"Sam was very clear about what he felt was best for him, he felt at the moment that no one is listening to him and this little boy's self belief and esteem may improve dramatically if consideration was seriously given to his opinion in the light of his future welfare.

Sam was very resistant to moving from the family home to a boarding school and it is clear that continuing legal procedures had resulted in Sam being very anxious about being away from the family that is supportive and caring . . ." She continued that, *"Court proceedings were having a very serious effect on Sam's mental health."*

Mrs Martins then wrote a separate note addressed to Joanne,

"Joanne, I am quite dismayed by the management of this case and it brings the law into disrepute. Perhaps we can have a brief word. Kindest regards . . ."

Mrs Martins also wrote a letter to Sam,

"Dear Sam,

Thank you so much for coming and working out all those questions and being so wonderful with the jigsaws and blocks.

You are a very talented boy and will make many beautiful objects in the future.

Please keep positive Sam. You are a very special boy and I feel certain that the legal proceedings will soon be finished.

Do keep enjoying your friends and Springer.

Yours affectionately . . ."

Joanne sent a copy to Elizabeth, who advised her that if Joanne was going to use the report at the next Court hearing, the report had to be disclosed to all parties beforehand.

When Gregory received a copy of the report he challenged its authenticity and wrote to Elizabeth, he believed that Joanne had dictated what Sam should write.

Elizabeth therefore wrote and asked Mrs Martins to clarify if Sam had written the piece independently and alone.

Mrs Martins was now getting the picture of what Joanne and Chris were up against. She sent a copy of Elizabeth's letter to Joanne with a hand written note saying,

"This whole sorry affair resembles a charade! I am quite shocked by the handling of this case: it brings the Courts into disrepute. I don't want to contact Elizabeth, can you send a copy of my note to her. Sorry about this Joanne. Mrs Martins."

The typed note then said,

"On the day that Sam was asked to produce information about himself Sam sat in the waiting room and provided this information.

This is the normal procedure for young patients so that they will be occupied during a formal meeting with the family.

The evidence of the timing of Sam's account has been questioned and there has been a suggestion that Sam's mother, Mrs Parry influenced the contents of Sam's report.

We are constantly surrounded by opinions from families, relatives, siblings and schools and the majority of children will adopt a selective memory so that what is meaningful and important to them will be recalled.

At the time of Sam's account of his feelings and thoughts, his mother was in a separate consulting room and Sam provided this information sitting at a table in the waiting room. So there is no evidence to indicate that she dictated her ideas to her son.

It is disappointing and distressing to hear that the evidence which Sam has provided has been subject to unkind and unwarranted criticism, which is wholly inappropriate."

Joanne could see that everything she produced was going to be challenged by Gregory and felt she would need more than Mrs Martins' report. If only she could make tape recordings of Sam's protests at having to go on visits and tape his 'phone conversations to Miss Graves, then maybe everyone could hear what was really going on.

Chris thought that recording everything certainly couldn't do any harm. He ordered the equipment and set up a recorder at the main telephone station in his study to tape all 'phone calls. Joanne told Sam that if he wanted to leave a message for Miss Graves in a way that she couldn't interrupt him, then maybe he should 'phone her after office hours and leave her a message. That way he could say exactly what he wanted.

The idea appealed to Sam. Being able to say just what you wanted to say without interruption seemed perfect!

He used the nights when he couldn't sleep to make the calls; Miss Graves had a direct line that she had instructed Sam to use, rather than the general office line. It would go straight to her 'phone she had assured Sam and only she would hear the message and he could call her at any time.

Sure enough, when Sam dialled the number, Miss Graves' voice came over the 'phone,

"This is the office of Miss Graves at CAFCASS, I'm not at my desk at the moment, but if you leave a message I'll deal with the matter on my return."

Sam waited until he heard the beep, then launched into his message,

"Look Miss Graves, its one o'clock in the morning and I can't sleep. I can't sleep because I can't help feeling that you are just not telling the Judge the truth. The truth is that I want to be with my mum and my brother and my pets. I don't want to have to go and see someone who they call my dad . . . anyway he's not my dad . . . and he doesn't act like my dad. It's my life and I want to live my life the way I want to live it. It's not up to you to tell me what to do. You tell me that your job is to tell the Judge my wishes and feelings. Well then. Please do your job and tell the silly old Judge . . . I'm gonna try and sleep now . . . and I want you to call me tomorrow and tell me that you are going to tell the Judge how I really feel."

The next message was from Miss Graves,

"I got your message Sam and I will tell the Judge what you said and put it in my report."

Sam felt proud of himself. He told Joanne that he had left several messages for Miss Graves and that he hoped that this time Miss Graves would listen to him.

Joanne listened to the tapes. There were four. Sam sounded quite confident at the beginning of his messages to Miss Graves, but as he got further into his message his little voice started to break into sobs and it brought a lump into Joanne's throat. This was what the Judge needed to hear, Sam was quite clear in his request.

All the messages were along the same lines. Joanne thought that now maybe she had enough evidence on the tapes to take to Court and present them to the Judge, along with a small tape recorder and earphones so that he could listen to them there and then.

At the next Court hearing Joanne presented Mrs Martins' report to Judge Sissens. As expected, Gregory got to his feet and told the Court that the report could not be relied upon; he said that Mrs Martins was a friend of Joanne's.

Well, that was a new excuse! But, thought Joanne, I suppose it wasn't too difficult to think that one up.

No matter. Joanne told the Judge that she had other similar evidence, but this time tape recordings of Sam's 'phone calls to Miss Graves. She handed the clerk the brown envelope containing the four tapes and recorder and the clerk passed it to Judge Sissens. He looked inside the envelope slightly bemused,

"This is unusual, but I surmise that I should listen to the tapes. I will see you all back in Court in an hour. Let us say twelve noon." Then Judge Sissens rose and left the Court.

At noon Joanne went back into the Courtroom. She was hopeful that this time the old guy would actually take note of what Sam had said.

As Joanne sat down on the Court bench she felt her mobile 'phone vibrate. She took the 'phone from her pocked and looked at the message. It was from Sam.

"Mum I'm here at the Court. I'm going to tell the Judge myself!"

Joanne felt proud of him. How had he got here? Maybe on his bicycle, but how would he find her?

Judge Sissens then entered the Court. Everyone rose, bowed and sat down again.

"Well," Judge Sissens pronounced, "I am truly astounded as to what lengths, you, Mrs Parry will go to. I am disgusted, that you, Mrs Parry, that you should treat the hard working Miss Graves in this disgraceful way. Astounded and disgusted. Appalled. Appalled that you should have made these recordings. I apologise to Miss Graves that she should be treated in this way and that her judgement that what is best for Sam has been questioned. I see Miss Graves is not here, but it will go on record that I said this."

Joanne got to her feet.

"My Lord. Sam is hear at Court to tell you himself, personally, if you will hear him."

"How dare you bring the child to Court. It is not permitted."

"I did *not* bring Sam to Court, he has just sent me a text message that he has come here by himself and he is somewhere in the building."

"This is outrageous!" Judge Sissens turned to the clerk, "Call Miss Graves's office and have the child taken care of, we can't have a child wondering about the Courts unattended. Give the tapes back to Mrs Parry," he commanded handing the brown envelope to the clerk, "I will see all persons concerned back here at two o'clock." Judge Sissens rose and left the Courtroom.

Joanne rushed out of the Courtroom and 'phoned Sam.

"Where are you? How did you get here?"

"I came on my bicycle. I'm at the main entrance to the Court."

"You're a clever boy. Lock your bike up safely and I'll come down and find you."

Joanne found Sam by the large gates at the entrance to the Court. She hugged him,

"Come and let me get you a hot chocolate in the Court canteen," she said and holding Sam's hand and she led him through the corridors to a small, brightly lit canteen. There were several people there, some dressed in pin-striped suits, others in black gowns, they were either carrying large bulging black brief cases or large bundles of typed sheets, neatly tied up in crimson ribbon. Joanne led Sam past the display of cold drinks and sandwiches and took her turn in the queue for hot drinks.

They found a table by the window with three chairs still free and sat there sipping their hot chocolate. They had only been there a few minutes when they were aware of a woman making her way towards their table. She stood out from the others because she was dressed casually in brown. Her coat was unbuttoned and showed a pretty rose coloured blouse over her brown skirt. Her greying brown hair, framed her friendly face and for a moment or two she paused and studied mother and son sitting at the table.

The Judge's clerk had 'phoned Miss Grave's office. Miss Graves was away; and as head of the department, Caroline Brume had to take responsibility. She had frantically searched through Miss Graves' desk. There was nothing in the files on Sam to suggest any problems. There were brief notes on meetings and interviews with Sam, but nothing controversial. There were no tapes of interviews or 'phone recordings, which were usually kept for evidence. If the tapes that had been presented to Court suggested a mishandling of the case, they would be hammered. If it leaked out, the media would have a field day!

Caroline approached the table where Joanne sat with Sam,

"You must be Mrs Parry . . . and is this Sam?" she asked smiling at Sam.

"Yes," said Joanne cautiously, wondering what was to happen next.

"May I sit with you a moment?" and she drew up the third chair. "My name is Caroline Brume I'm from CAFCASS and this . . ." she said turning round to a man making his way towards the table, "is my colleague, Jonathan Davis, a child psychiatrist."

Joanne swallowed hard and felt for Sam's hand. Now what! She looked up at Jonathan; he looked friendly enough. He was also dressed in a brown coat, his dark curly hair falling informally about his face.

Caroline turned towards Sam and said,

"Sam, do you mind if I have a little chat with your Mum? Your Mum and I will sit just over there next to the other window, so that you can still see us and Jonathan will keep you company."

Caroline led Joanne to the other table and sat down looking deeply into her face.

"I understand that you have some tapes that you showed to the Judge."

"Yes," said Joanne. She clutched the slim computer bag that Chris had given her to keep her papers and tapes together.

"May I see the tapes?"

"Surely you must have copies of these 'phone calls at your offices. Anyway, I don't understand who you are and why you are here."

"I'm sorry. I should explain. Miss Graves is away on holiday. I am her manager."

"I didn't know Miss Graves had a manager!"

"Yes she does. She has to answer to me! I have looked through Sam's file and there are no records of any 'phone calls."

Joanne reached into the black computer bag and pulled out the brown envelope containing the tapes and the little recorder and ear 'phones.

"Well they are here. You can listen to them if you like. I have copies," she added anxiously, "but I'd like to have the originals back."

"Don't worry. I'm not going to take them away. I just want to listen to them here."

Caroline flicked though the tapes, sometimes fast-forwarding, sometimes rewinding to hear bits again.

"I've got other recordings as well . . . at home," said Joanne and suddenly the words came tumbling out, "I've got tape recordings of the 'phone calls Gregory made to Sam . . . you can hear Sam crying, begging Gregory not to collect him. Miss Graves refused to listen to the tapes. Chris, that's my husband, also recorded Sam protesting, refusing to go out of the house to Gregory's car, he was crying saying why did he have to, it was his life, no one else's, why did he have to go? Sam begged Miss Graves to tell the Judge that he didn't want to go on visits and how much he dreaded them. He said that if she was really his solicitor, then she should tell this old fashioned Judge; Sam's words not mine," added Joanne, "that no one is going to ruin any more of his life, he wanted his life back, it was his life and he had to live it." Now the tears were welling up in Joanne's eyes as she remembered how distressed Sam had been and how helpless she had felt to prevent his suffering.

Caroline patted Joanne's hand trying to comfort her.

"May I have a quick word with Sam? I just need him to verify that it is his voice on the tapes."

Joanne pulled herself together,

"Yes, of course!"

Caroline made her way back to where Sam was sitting with Jonathan.

"Sam," she smiled, "may I sit here and show you something? Maybe ask you a few questions?"

Caroline sat next to Sam and showed him the tapes.

"Do you know what these are?" she asked looking closely at Sam. Sam shook his head, slightly bemused.

"They are tape recordings of the 'phone calls that you made to Miss Graves . . . at night when you couldn't sleep. Did you know your Mum was taping your 'phone conversations?"

Sam shook his head again.

"Will you listen to the tapes for me and tell me if it is you on the tapes or someone else?"

Sam nodded. He put the ear 'phones into his ears and Caroline started the tape.

"Yes! That's me," said Sam earnestly. "She would *never* listen to me!" His frustration mounting, "she just kept saying I had to see my dad . . . but he's not my dad . . . and anyway all he does is make my life miserable . . . she said she would tell the Judge . . . but she never did."

Sam looked up distraughtly at Caroline. He had had enough of all these grownups pretending to help him, but who never did. No one ever saw it from his point of view.

"Now I'm going to fetch your Mum. I think you both need another hot chocolate and something to eat. Then you will need to stay here with Jonathan while I go to see the Judge with your Mum. Don't worry, we'll work something out."

She motioned to Joanne to come and sit with Sam and then said to her, "I need to go back to my offices and prepare some papers for the Judge. I'll see you back in Court."

At two o'clock Joanne and Caroline were back in Court.

Judge Sissens made his usual entrance, then when seated, he announced:

"I understand from Miss Brume's report that Miss Graves is moving on to further pastures and that in the meantime, Miss Brume, you and your colleague Jonathan Davis will be overseeing Sam's welfare."

Phew! Thought Joanne. At long last Miss Graves has been taken off the job.

Judge Sissens droned on:

"I wish Miss Graves the very best in her future work. It is a pity that she is not here so that I can thank her for all her assistance in this case. No doubt her colleague will pass on my thanks to her and of course, this will be in the Court records."

Now, thought Joanne, how cunning is that!

So all that is on the Court recordings is that Joanne was to blame. Joanne had acted disgracefully and treated Miss Graves so badly that she had voluntarily moved to another job and how grateful Judge Sissens was for Miss Graves' most excellent work in this case! What a farce! Why is the truth not broadcasted? That Miss Graves was found out by her manager, that

Miss Graves had concealed or destroyed records of the 'phone calls Sam made to her. In other words, failed to protect Sam, failed to do her job and was now sacked!

Miss Brume then stood up and said:

"My Lord, I think that maybe it is appropriate that Sam be considered to be allowed his own solicitor and barrister to represent him in Court. Sam is nearly thirteen years old and mature enough to make his views known. May I also suggest that for Sam's sake the matter of paternity should be clarified and I suggest a DNA test be done by Cellmark Diagnostics Limited which is approved by the Court?"

Judge Sissens pondered on Miss Brume's suggestions and then said:

"Very well Miss Brume, if that is your considered opinion, that Sam should have his own solicitor, then I welcome it. As far as the DNA is concerned, I will leave it to you to make the necessary arrangements." Judge Sissens rose from his grand chair and turned and left the Court.

"All rise!" shouted the clerk.

φ

It was a few weeks later that Joanne was walking home after having dropped Alex off at one of his friends for a play day, when Elizabeth called her on her mobile,

"I've some good news for a change!" She said enthusiastically, "It's official! Gregory is not the father!

I have the papers in my hand! It came by post today. You should have a copy at home too!"

So the fertility clinic *had* slipped up, thought Joanne, *or* wanted to improve their statistics, or maybe they felt sorry for her and had made as near a match to her colouring as possible. Whatever the reason, it was now fact.

ϕ

Joanne was overjoyed. A sudden rush of excitement went through her. She felt free. She wanted to fly through the air, she was just so happy, so relieved. Sam was her son and her son alone. Gregory was not Sam's father.

At last Joanne could see a glimmer of light at the end of the tunnel. Now, thought Joanne, now is the time to go the whole way, pull out all the stops and she thought of just the man to call.

Meanwhile, Sam was at Gregory's. He sat at the kitchen table, dutifully eating his pasta and tomato soup. Concentrating on his pasta was a good excuse to be pre-occupied and not to have to look at Gregory while he lectured Sam about boarding school. Gregory said that he had visited the school; it was nice; out in the country with lots of space. He told Sam that boarding school would be good for him.

Sam didn't answer him; he just stared at his pasta, twiddling it about with his fork, deep in thought. Who *was* this man? He didn't *look* like Sam. He didn't *think* like Sam. They had *nothing* in common and now he wanted to send him away. Away from his mum! Away from his brother and his pets!

Sam finished his pasta, angrily pushed back his chair from the table and without a word he turned his back on Gregory and stomped out of the room. He strode upstairs to his bedroom and quickly sent Joanne a text message.

"Mum I've had enough. I can't cope with any more visits. I want to come home!"

Joanne could not resist replying with the good news,

"Dearest Sam, you needn't worry any more. Gregory is not your father. You are free. Love you x miss you x Mum xxxx."

φ

"You did what?" exclaimed Elizabeth incredulously, "You told Sam the news that Gregory is not his father *in a text message!* The Judge is not going to like that!"

"Why not? What's the problem? It's the news we've all being waiting for. Sending text messages is today's way of communication. Sam needed the confirmation as soon as possible. He needed to be put him out of his misery, to know that *that* man can no longer have a hold over him."

"Yes, well, Judges are a bit old fashioned. He's not going to like this."

"Well how's he going to know?"

"Oh don't you doubt it! Somebody will tell him!

Then Elizabeth went on to say thoughtfully, "You know Joanne, for Sam's sake you should try and find out who the real father is. Sam needs to know his genetic background, you should write to the clinic and see if they can dig out the records."

Joanne found out that Professor Churchill had moved his clinic from the local hospital, where he had occupied the whole of the fifth floor, to a four storey private town house that he had renovated to suit his clinical requirements. Professor Churchill's secretary replied to Joanne's letter, saying that the old medical records had been archived at the hospital and that the only records that they kept at the clinic were from the last seven years. She suggested to Joanne that she should contact the hospital security officer and ask him to locate her records.

The hospital security officer didn't respond to Joanne's letters, he seemed to be only part time and semi-retired. Joanne was used to getting the answer 'phone whenever she called his number, then one afternoon she was halfway through cooking a spicy sauce to go with the evening dinner, when he answered the 'phone. She turned the heat off the stove and sat down at the kitchen table to concentrate on what he had to say.

He explained that when Professor Churchill moved out of the hospital, all the old records had been deposited in the hospital basement in huge cardboard boxes, because there had not been sufficient room to house them at his new clinic. Since then the hospital had had a flood in the basement and now most of the paperwork was destroyed or indecipherable. There was really nothing he could do. Joanne would need to get permission to look through what had survived the flood, but the task of going through partly destroyed boxes would be huge and would probably take months, if not years and there was no guarantee of finding anything useful. Joanne put the 'phone down just as Sam walked into the kitchen and flung his school satchel down on the floor. He looked round at Joanne.

"Hey mum! What's up? You look a bit down," he said walking towards her and put his arms affectionately around her shoulders.

"I was just trying to find out who your real dad was. To see if the clinic or the hospital could trace the records for you," she said looking up at Sam.

Sam stepped back from her, "Oh mum! No! No! Please! No way! Even if you *did* find out, I don't want to know! I do *not want* to know! I've been through enough! I could *not* go through anything like I've been through, not ever again! Not ever! What happens if my real dad is as mad as Mr Franks? No way! I'm happy here, where I am." Sam came forward and put his arms around Joanne's shoulders and kissed her cheek, "I have you mum and I have Chris. That is all I ever want!"

Chapter Ten

Fast Forward to 2003

The Breakthrough!

Elizabeth's children needed more space and she decided to move out into the country and join another practice. She suggested to Joanne that she find another solicitor in town, someone easy to access.

Matthew was the solicitor who had helped Joanne with the original divorce proceedings so she decided to call him for advice. She explained that she needed somebody who was bold enough to jump outside the box of protocols and do something wild and different. Joanne was sure she had a case; she was sure that she was right and that right would prevail.

"Well, it will cost you!" Matthew said. "I know just the person. But she's expensive!"

"They're all expensive!" groaned Joanne, "You're saying that it's a woman? Will she be able to do as well as a man?"

"Oh, this lady is different. Believe me. She stops at nothing!"

Well that was all Joanne needed to hear. She and Chris would find the money somehow.

To save time, Joanne carefully sifted through the papers to keep the bundle as concise as possible. But some copies of the Court Orders were missing. She realised that she had better go to the Court office and request photocopies.

Joanne went through the usual painful process of security at the Court entrance and was then directed through a door at one side of the main hall. There was an old wooded sign nailed to the wall with a man's hand carved on it with a long finger pointing to the right. Joanne followed the directions and walked down the corridor. Then another wooden sign, with another long finger, pointed down some old stone steps with a wooden banister rail supported on wrought iron railings. Joanne carefully walked down the narrow steps. It felt cold and damp; like going into a dungeon, thought Joanne, but if that's what you have to do, better get on with it.

The steps stopped abruptly and another long finger pointed to the left, down yet another narrow corridor, but then the corridor ended with a blank wall. Joanne turned round confused, then discovered that inserted in one of the walls was some tall wooden panelling reaching up to the ceiling. The ceiling was interesting; it was arched as you might find in a cellar. Joanne looked along the panelled wall and in it was concealed a small shallow counter with a sliding panel. To the right of the counter was a small black button and a little black notice with white lettering with the words printed, "press for assistance".

Joanne pressed the black button. After a while the wooden panel was drawn aside and there was Aedan, as she had come to know him. He was Irish with only one good arm, the other one he didn't seem to use and he was always so kind and helpful.

Aeden smiled broadly when he saw Joanne.

"Hello Joanne! Ye see they've moved us down here now," he explained. The clerks were not meant to tell people their names, but he knew Joanne's name from the top of the files.

"Yes! I was a bit puzzled when I was directed here, it's not as nice as the other offices" she commented.

"I see you're due back in Court again Miss Joanne," he looked at her sympathetically, "it's still going on then! Not finished yet?"

"No," she sighed resignedly, "not yet!"

"Ye know, it's the longest running case in the history of this place ye know?" he went on, "the *largest* number of files. It fills the place . . . never seen anything like it . . . it takes several of us to wheel this lot over to the Courts, ye know . . ."

Aedan took Joanne's list of the Court Orders that she needed. She explained that she had most of them, but some were missing from her files. Aedan dutifully disappeared among the rows of shelves and then reappeared some time later with a bundle of papers, which he photocopied and handed them to her.

"I wish ye luck Missy, you deserve some luck . . . ye don't give up, do ye?" he said, looking at her admiringly.

As she walked away down the corridor, Aedan called after her:

"I wish ye all the luck . . . all the luck in the world . . . don't give up!"

As Joanne hugged the bundle of papers, she realised that all their hopes now rested in this new blunderbuss. This would have to be the last stand. They were seriously short of funds.

φ

Margery Bordon was her name, a composed and purposeful woman, probably in her late forties with short dark hair. Her glasses made her look stern and business-like and she certainly had no time for small talk.

The meeting at her office had been brief. Just long enough to be introduced, to hand over the bundle of papers Joanne had prepared and to sign the usual agreement on fees.

"You need to find Sam his own solicitor," advised Margery, "I'll give you a list of recommended solicitors who are experienced in dealing with children and family matters. It will be done on Legal Aid of course and this all takes time, so I suggest you get cracking! In the meantime I will look out a QC to take on your case. Mr Franks is not the father and we need to know if there is any mileage in the fact that Sam was born before the Children's Act came into force. I know the gentleman I'd like to instruct, it's all a matter of whether he is free to take on Sam's case."

Joanne found that looking for a solicitor to represent Sam at relatively short notice was not easy. There were only a few weeks before the Hearing in March and everybody seemed to be booked up. Joanne worked through Margery's list but each time Joanne made an enquiry, she was simply passed on to the next company of solicitors.

Eventually Joanne tried calling a Miss George whose offices were not too far from Sam's school. She was away on compassionate leave and her cases had been postponed or taken over by colleagues. She was due back to work at the end of January and her secretary said that she might be prepared to take on Sam's case since there had been a necessary lull in her workload. Joanne left a message for Miss George, imploring her to take on Sam's case. Her secretary explained that Miss George would not be able to have any contact with Joanne. If Miss George took on Sam's case, she would be his personal solicitor and that Sam would meet with her and her Counsel to prepare Sam's statement, under his instruction and his instruction alone. Well, it sounded reasonably promising, it seemed that no one could interfere with what Sam wanted to put in his statement, or so Joanne thought.

A few days later Sam got a letter from Miss George's secretary saying that she was happy to take on Sam's case and that she proposed a meeting with Sam and Counsel at her offices.

Sam felt very grown up at having Miss George as his own solicitor and Miss Campbell as his Counsel. Both Miss George and Miss Campbell seemed about the same age, Sam thought they were probably in their thirties, but they seemed very experienced. When he was with them he felt he was with friends, they were on his side. He thought Miss Campbell was particularly pretty; she had dark brown eyes that sparkled against her pale freckled skin, her brown wavy hair framed her face and the only makeup seemed to be an orangey colour on her lips. Miss George appeared a bit more serious with a pair of dark rimmed glasses which she liked to wear half-way down her nose, Sam thought this was probably to make her look more intellectual. Above all, Sam felt that things could now get better and he began to feel positive about the whole thing.

Miss George carefully interviewed Sam, while Miss Campbell listened and took notes; they wanted to make sure Sam was mature enough to understand the consequences of what he might want to tell the Court.

Sam had several meetings with them, which had taken place after school. At that time of the afternoon it was getting dark, so Joanne arranged for Sam to be picked up from school by taxi and taken directly to Miss George's offices. That way he would not be walking the streets in the dark. Also, no one could say that Joanne had collected Sam from school and primed him with what to say to Miss George.

Sam felt quite grown up being collected from the school gates by taxi. He handed the driver a note of the address he was to be taken to and settled back on the back seat with his thoughts. At school Sam was happy, he was able to immerse himself in his schoolwork and have fun with his school friends; Court seemed a million miles away. But in the taxi, on the way to Miss George's offices, the gloom outside made all the anxious feelings come rushing back.

Once he was in Miss George's office he felt as if a weight had been taken off his shoulders, a positive feeling that at last he could tell her how he truly felt, what he really wanted and it felt good. He was fed up of confiding in his so-called representative, who would try to persuade Sam what was good for him, try to persuade him to do things he didn't want to do. The air seemed clearer now; he needn't waste his time explaining his views to people who weren't listening. It gave Sam a feeling of confidence that he had not felt before.

Miss Graves's questions had always seemed as if they had come from Gregory himself, as though Gregory had dictated them to her. The questions only seemed to benefit Gregory, not Sam. But Miss George was different, she listened to him and she seemed to understand him. She explained that not everything would be possible, but she would do her best to fight for what he wanted.

Sam impressed Miss George and Miss Campbell. He was not yet thirteen, but he was very articulate and knew just what he wanted. He would look earnestly at them, his blue eyes looking boldly into theirs. Occasionally, when considering something, he would lower his head and comb his fingers through his wiry blond hair, then look up and say exactly what he wanted to achieve. Sometimes Miss George would 'phone Sam when she wanted further clarification on a point, but otherwise it all seemed straight forward as she prepared a statement on his behalf.

φ

Joanne was clearing the breakfast table when she heard the fax machine churning out documents in the study. What now, she thought and went upstairs to the study and pulled the paper off the machine. It was yet *another* Court Order! Great! So now instead of a few days notice by post, Court Orders were being faxed through direct. Joanne read down the page.

"Mr Gregory Franks do have leave to give short notice to Mrs Joanne Parry of his application for the child to take an exam at Clarendon Boarding School. The said application will be listed before Mr Justice Sissens at the Durford Law Court on February 9, not before twelve noon."

But that's today! Joanne could not believe it. Talk about short notice. She looked at her watch. Nine o'clock. Was it really worth trying to get there? Wherever Durford was, she hadn't a clue. So that was Gregory's latest game. Get Joanne dashing all over the country to whichever Court he happened to be in and hope she couldn't get there in time to be heard. If Joanne didn't turn up then an Order would be made in her absence and she would have no say in the matter.

Chris, as usual, was a tower of strength. He printed out Mrs Martins' report and gave Joanne one of his portable computers with all the files loaded on it. He looked up the train times to Durford, saw Sam and Alex off to school, before rushing off to work at the hospital.

He kissed Joanne goodbye and hugged her tightly, holding her hard against his chest. He wanted to try and inject some strength and determination and make her feel supported and loved.

The train journey had seemed to take forever. Joanne could not relax. She bought a magazine and flicked through it, she went through her papers, she bought herself a coffee, but the restlessness she felt, wouldn't leave her.

At last she stood in the queue for a taxi, she shivered and held up her umbrella to protect her from the February rain. Joanne wished she'd put on a warm coat over her black suit, her feet were cold in her black high heels and boots would have been more practical, but she had to look the part when she got to Court. She must look business-like; it was essential.

Settling herself in the back seat of the taxi, Joanne asked the driver, "How far is it to Durford County Court?"

"About twenty minutes. What time have you got to be there?"

"Before twelve noon!"

"No problem, I'll have you there by eleven-forty."

The Courthouse looked quite modern from the outside. A large building in pale sandstone, with big oak doors and large glass panes, through which it was possible to see people walking to and fro in their dark uniforms.

Joanne paid the taxi driver and thanked him for getting her there so quickly. She walked up the stone steps to the entrance and pushed open the heavy oak doors to be greeted by the usual security system that was by now familiar to her and just part and parcel of the whole experience. Once over that hurdle she made her way down the main hallway, her high heels making a loud clicking noise on the stone floors. The building looked more like a theatre. Well, thought Joanne, she supposed that was what it was in a way! Off the large hallway were lots of doors and a dark carpeted staircase led up to a gallery.

Joanne walked up the stairs, paused at the top and looked about her. There were rows of chairs covered in a hardwearing dark cloth. People sat talking to each other in hushed tones. Some were going through files of papers, some had computers. Some were dressed similarly to herself; others were barristers who walked past in their wigs and gowns, carrying papers under their arms. Joanne saw the Court timetable pinned to one of the wooden pillars. Yes, her name was listed there; not before noon. Well, that could mean anytime really, she would just have to find herself a seat and wait. Joanne felt alone. How much longer would all this go on? How much longer could she keep it up? She saw a free seat and was about to sit down when she saw a bustling group of people emerge in the dim light at the top of the stairs. They looked anxiously around the poorly lit waiting area. One of ladies in the group pointed to Joanne and whispered to her colleague,

"There she is!"

It was Margery. She too had received a fax that morning and she was not going to be out done by Gregory's manoeuvers, she had also informed Miss George and Miss Campbell to be there on Sam's behalf.

"Not to be out done!" Margery said firmly as she approached Joanne, "I'm getting a bit fed up with this man, it's got to stop! He's gone one step too far this time." Margery held out a roll of fax paper, "Twenty seven pages of this stuff! Absolute drivel! And all at the last minute!" She went on, "It's actually not worth reading. Best just to stick to the case in point! I doubt that we'll be heard before lunch so let's go get something in the canteen and discuss matters. The clerks will find us if they need us. They know we're here. I have informed them at the desk."

In the Court canteen Margery and Joanne sipped coffee as they discussed what was likely to happen.

"Miss George and Miss Campbell are here today too, as Sam's solicitor and counsel. I think Gregory's application to send Sam to boarding school can be safely quashed. Our case is that the Court should wait for Sam's official Statement before there are any more Court Orders," advised Margery.

"Case of Parry and Franks," called out a clerk.

"Gosh! That was quick!" said Margery in surprise. They quickly gathered up their papers and made their way to the Courtroom.

In Court, Gregory had persuaded one of his friends, a QC, to act for him. He made two applications; one to have it established that Sam's mental health should be questioned and therefore Sam's Statement should not be relied on, that he could state things that he did not really mean, or understand. The second application was for Sam to attend an interview with the headmaster of Clarendon Boarding School.

Judge Sissens planned to retire next year and he was keen to see an end to this case. He was beginning to feel weary with the numerous applications, usually done at short notice and felt that they were really not well thought through.

Judge Sissens ordered that firstly there should be no more applications until Sam's Statement was heard and secondly that before the final Court hearing in March, Sam's solicitor should arrange a meeting between

Mr Franks and Sam and that the meeting should include an interview at Clarendon Boarding School.

Joanne was aghast! Even the experienced Margery was stunned at such an Order. It showed the blatant determination of Judge Sissens to allow Gregory to have his way. But at the same time it gave Margery an understanding of what Joanne and Sam were up against. Judge Sissens and Gregory were obviously not going to give up, despite Sam having his own solicitor. Judge Sissens had given his instructions and the Order had to be obeyed.

Walking down the corridor, away from the Courtroom, Miss George and Miss Campbell put their heads together and conversed in low tones. Margery saw them and decided to offer some advice,

"If there is to be a meeting between Sam and Mr Franks, may I suggest that it is done at your offices and that you take the precaution of taping the meeting? You will need to make it clear to Sam that if at any point he wishes to finish the meeting or leave the room, then he is free to do so and that nobody will interfere or try to stop him."

"Don't worry," responded Miss George gravely, "we had already thought of that, 'though we feel that Sam would need a lot of persuading!"

Two weeks later a letter arrived addressed to Sam. On the reverse of the envelope, it stated that if not delivered, please return to Fleet Road. Joanne recognised the address as being that of Miss George's offices. She left the letter on Sam's bedside table for when he came home after school.

That evening, Joanne asked Sam if he would mind if she saw what was in the letter. It seemed odd that Miss George should write to Sam, when she could 'phone him at any time or have him go to her offices. Joanne wondered why she should write to Sam. Perhaps she was writing to in the hope that maybe Sam would show the letter to Joanne. That would be the natural thing, for Sam to show his mother what might be a formal letter that may not be so easily understood.

Miss George had written to Sam explaining that she had written to Judge Sissens and enclosed a copy of letter she had written to the Judge's clerk,

"Dear Madam,

I am writing further to the Order made by Judge Sissens in this case on February 9.

On that date His Lordship ordered, that as Sam's solicitor, I should make arrangements for a meeting between Sam and the Respondent, Mr Franks, such meeting to include a visit to Clarendon Boarding School.

I am writing to inform His Lordship of the current position and to seek his guidance in respect of the future conduct of his matter in the period leading up to the hearing in March.

I have met with Sam on several occasions both on my own and in conference with Miss Campbell of Counsel. I have also spoken with Sam on the telephone.

Counsel and I have carefully explained to Sam exactly what took place on February 9, the Orders that His Lordship make in respect of the arrangements for the meeting with Mr Franks and the reasons His Lordship gave for making the Orders.

I made it clear on the occasions I met with Sam that he should not make any decision now and that he should think over

what we had discussed. In conference with Counsel it was clear that Sam had considered carefully what had been proposed and the consequences of his instruction to us.

Sam has said that he will not meet Mr Franks because he is quite sure this will not achieve anything. He has tried to do this before and feels Mr Franks has never taken any of the things he has said on board. Sam is very distressed at the moment, is under stress and does not want to have anything to do with Mr Franks.

Sam is adamant that he does not want to discuss the entrance exam for Clarendon Boarding School or any other school, or his future schooling with Mr Franks and that he does not wish contact with Mr Franks.

In the circumstances and in the context of the Orders made by His Lordship I should be very grateful for His Lordship's guidance in respect of the conduct of this matter."

So Miss George was doing her best for Sam. Judge Sissens had put pressure on her to persuade Sam to meet with Gregory, but she was firmly telling Judge Sissens what Sam's feelings were in the matter and that he could not be persuaded otherwise.

The following morning Margery's secretary 'phoned to tell Joanne and Chris that she had been successful in arranging a meeting with the Q.C. of her choice. This was to consider whether Sam's case should fall outside the Children's Act of 1991.

φ

Tall and good looking, he was young, probably thirty five or so, which seemed a slight mismatch with the old fashioned grey pin-stripped suit that he was wearing. Mr Charles had to be pretty bright to become a QC so young. Margery had said that he had done some high profile child cases, but of course Joanne and Chris would not have heard of them, as this sort of thing did not reach the headlines—only the law reports.

The room was not exactly stuffy, but the tall ceilings, elegant windows, shelves of law books and the traditional mahogany furniture of the conference room, seemed at odds with the real world outside.

Staring out of the window Joanne could see the new green grass on the elegant lawns, the trees coming into leaf. Everything looked new, hopeful, fresh. Yet inside, in this cloistered, almost Dickensian room with its fusty books, it felt suspended in time.

Mr Charles carefully turned the pages of the huge, red, law book, slowly pondering over the words. It seemed like an age, when at last he looked up at Joanne and Chris and announced,

"I think you have a case!"

"Wonderful!" blurted out Joanne. Chris looked at her as though to say: "don't rush it."

Mr Charles continued,

"Sam was born the year before the Children's Act of 1991 came into force and it states that the Act cannot be applied retrospectively."

Joanne couldn't resist saying,

"So what are waiting for? The Judge is wrong to make Sam visit Gregory!"

Mr Charles looked up at her and said in a measured way:

"It's a matter of *persuading* the Judge of that!"

φ

Mr Charles was right. Standing in Court, in his most formal manner, Mr Charles begged his Lordship to hear the relevant paragraph. The Judge listened and after a long silence, he lifted his head and looked straight back at Mr Charles,

"And *how*, Mr Charles, does *that* help *this* case?"

It was unbelievable. *Why* did the Judge insist on ignoring this?

The eightieth Court hearing was held on a sunny March morning, but inside the huge Courtroom it felt cold and austere; the dark wood panelling lined the sides of the Courtroom and seemed to separate everyone from the world outside. There were hard wooden benches to sit on and everything seemed very antiquated. Two clerks in their black gowns pottered here and there arranging papers and glasses of water for the Judge.

On the front row of benches to the right of the Court sat Gregory with his QC. They huddled together keeping their backs to the rest of the room, as they conversed with each other. Mr Charles seated himself two rows behind on the other side of the Court to the left. Joanne was told to sit on the row immediately behind Mr Charles so they could speak to each other when necessary. Chris sat next to Joanne, then Margery, as instructing solicitor, then Sam's barrister Miss Campbell and Miss George, her instructing solicitor. Sam was not allowed in Court and he had to remain at home, but Miss Campbell held in her hand his statement that was to be read out.

"All rise!" commanded the clerk, as Judge Sissens emerged from a Court door to the right of his high bench, wearing the familiar gray wig and bright red gown and he took his place in front of his grand chair. He faced the Court and everyone dutifully bowed. Then, after Judge Sissens had seated himself, everyone else sat down.

Gregory's QC opened the case. As usual, Gregory's tactics were to make complaints and to waste as much of the available Court time as possible, rather than to get to the point of the hearing. He knew that time in Court, with solicitors and QCs in attendance, cost a lot of money and if the Court did not get through the hearing on that day, another day would have to be booked. Gregory's QC represented Gregory for free, the state was paying for Miss Campbell because Sam was a minor, but for Joanne and Chris the outlay for Mr Charles and Margery was huge.

First Gregory's QC protested at the presence of Miss Campbell who represented Sam, which took up the first hour of the proceedings. Judge Sisssens knew that he was obliged to give Gregory's QC time to have his say, or he could be criticised for not allowing a full hearing.

Gregory's QC complained that Gregory knew Sam's barrister because she had appeared against him in another hearing.

Judge Sissens declared that he too knew Miss Campbell well; he knew her to do a good job and that she should be trusted to carry out her duty.

Miss Campbell, dressed in a smart dark gray suit and crisp white blouse, stood up and held her papers in front of her. Joanne held her breath. She knew how Sam felt, but what had he actually put in his Statement? What was he prepared to say to the Court?

Miss Campbell cleared her throat and began to read out, what she called, the Position Statement, on behalf of Sam.

"1. *Sam asks the Court,*" she said firmly, " *to put a stop to Mr Franks interfering in his life and in particular, his education. A residence order in favour of his mother and Chris Parry would give legal effect to what he considers his family unit. He asked the Court to place on record that Mr Franks was not his biological father.*

2. There have been proceedings for as long as Sam can remember. The bundles before the Court contain documents relating to 80 Court hearings, 26 hearings in just the last three years. Since 1996 Sam has been seen/interviewed/assessed by educational therapists, Court Welfare Officers, Clinical Psychologists, Consultants in Child and Adolescent Psychiatry, Educational Psychologists, therapists . . ."

Sam's statement went on to name all the people who had written reports on him, the different schools he had attended and all the Court hearings he had endured and then came the summing up.

Miss Campbell concluded:

3. The result has been interference and disruption in his life, in particular his schooling and the situation for him has got worse, not better.

Sam believes that if Mr Franks remains in the picture there will always be problems. He feels that Mr Franks will obstruct any further attempts he makes to go to another school. Sam does not miss Mr Franks and has been able to get on with his life and been more settled at school. The only thing that upsets his life is when a hearing comes up.

Sam is clear about and has thought through, the consequences of his decision and states that he is the person who has got to live the life ahead of him. Mr Franks must understand that Sam has had enough and does not want any contact direct, or indirect with him and does not wish contact with Mr Franks in the future."

Miss Campbell then sat down. She had done her bit.

Gregory lent over to his QC and whispered instructions to him. The QC got to his feet and with hands clasped behind his back, he rocked to and fro on his toes as he started his speech. He challenged Sam's statement, he said that Sam was not mentally stable and therefore Sam's statement could not be relied on.

Joanne's heart sank. What would Judge Sissens make of that? More delays?

Judge Sissens stood up,

"I'll see everyone back in Court at two o'clock," he said bluntly and he turned his back, swishing his red gown behind him as he left the Court.

"All rise!" shouted the clerk quickly.

At two o'clock everyone assembled back in the Courtroom for Judge Sissens to deliver his summing up. Sam's future depended on what the Judge ordered. Everything was at stake. Joanne had been told that no one wins a Court case. The Judge's main aim was to make sure there was no leeway for an appeal; that was the Judge's ultimate goal, he had to make sure that Gregory was satisfied.

On the left of the Courtroom Joanne took her place on the bench seat next to Chris and slipped her hand into his. This was it, the final Judgement.

Mr Charles sat in front of them with his books and files and Miss Campbell sat alongside with Miss George. Gregory and his QC kept to the front far right of the Courtroom.

Judge Sissens had ten pages of A4 notes to read in his summing up and he certainly took his time about it. He had written out the whole history of the case and tortuously droned on and on about this and that and of course, all the time sympathising with poor Mr Franks.

Joanne's attention was drawn when Judge Sissens mentioned a letter that he had received from Joanne. She had asked the Judge to order Gregory to allow Sam to go to his school friend's family home in Hong Kong. Judge Sissens recalled that the letter recounted how Gregory Franks had refused to give his permission. Judge Sissens suddenly raised his voice and bellowed:

"That is not fair. That is simply not a true representation of Mr Franks' position!"

What *is* he talking about? Thought Joanne. It was a requirement by the Court that both parents have to approve a child leaving the country. Joanne had to go to Court to get permission to over-ride Gregory's refusal. Judge Sissens had been away on holiday and Joanne remembered how she and Chris had taken Sam to the Court annex where small matters were heard by the Judge of the day. In the small annex Courtroom there had just been Judge Cullen with his assistant. Joanne and Chris had presented the invitation from Tom's parent and the duty social worker had interviewed Sam and put forward Sam's point of view that he regarded the invitation as a trip of a lifetime. Gregory had explained to Judge Cullen that Sam wouldn't go places with *him*, so why should he allow *Sam* to go places with his friends! Judge Cullen shook his head and advised Mr Franks that he should think carefully about his objection to Sam's trip and that he should reconsider his decision.

So why was Judge Sissens denying that Gregory had objected to Sam's trip? What was the point? To try and make out that Joanne had made it up?

Judge Sissens continued on his theme of putting Joanne down,

"I have in mind, in particular, the most *disgraceful* way that Mrs Parry treated Miss Graves . . . and there is the CAFCASS bill that shall be shared equally between Mrs Parry and Mr Franks.

After that *appalling* episode, leave was given for Sam to instruct a solicitor and counsel of his own. I am by no means thought to regard Mr Franks as an ideal parent, or to have conducted himself in a fashion which could be described as ideal."

Oh well, I guess that's at least *something*, thought Joanne and she listened as he continued,

"One reason Sam mentioned more than once to the professionals for not wanting anything to do with Mr Franks and I have recognised that there were others, is Sam's resentment of what he sees as the part that Mr Franks played in removing him from St Luke's.

In 2001 Mr Franks arranged, without the mother's consent, for Sam to be assessed to go to a special needs school, the mother suggested two other schools should be considered for entry in 2003. It is a distortion of the truth that Mr Franks was the effective mover of the change of school because you, Mrs Parry agreed it."

Joanne stood up and cried out,

"No I did not!"

"Yes you did! You agreed it! It's recorded in the transcripts. I read from the transcripts in front of me, that you, Mrs Parry, having spoken to the headmaster, said that Sam had no place at St Luke's."

Joanne refused to be bullied, she persisted with her point,

"Sam had no place at St Luke's because Mr Franks had removed him from St Luke's!"

Mr Charles turned round in his seat to face Joanne and motioned her to sit down and not make a fuss. It seemed that Mr Charles was looking at the bigger picture, the outcome of all this, not the detail.

"But Gregory removed Sam from St Luke's," whispered Joanne to Mr Charles, "*how can* Judge Sissens *say* this? *How can* he get away with it?"

Despondently Joanne sank back into her seat. This was just *so, so* unfair. How much further from the truth could it get? Gregory had cancelled the contract with St Luke's, even though Sam was only eleven and still had two more years to go there. Elizabeth had tried to get a protection order to prevent Gregory from interfering with Sam's education at St Luke's, but it seemed hard to achieve, as long as Mr Franks remained an 'interested party'. In the end, Edward Williams didn't want any more the harassment, he had his school to run and the whole affair was too stressful to handle.

Joanne thought back to that Court hearing when Joanne had begged Judge Gibbons to talk to Edward Williams himself, or to ask him to come to Court. But no, Judge Gibbons had ordered Joanne to go *outside* the Courtroom and 'phone Edward Williams to verify the position. Of course, thought Joanne, that way the actual 'phone conversation was not recorded in Court. If the 'phone call had been made in the Courtroom for all to hear, then the Court records would have revealed the truth.

How clever! Judge Sissens was relying on the Court records for his summing up.

Joanne feverishly rummaged through the papers she had brought to Court with her. She remembered recently seeing an old invoice from Elizabeth detailing just this event and a bill for all the letters she'd written pleading with Mr Edwards to keep Sam at St Lukes and letters sent to Gregory Franks asking him not to interfere with St Luke's any more.

Yes! She found the invoice and tapped Mr Charles on the shoulder, he turned round to her and she slipped the invoice into his hand for him to read.

Mr Charles scanned the invoice details, then stood up,

"I hesitate to interrupt Your Lordship's Judgement. My Lord, there is the matter that I can tell Your Lordship at this stage, about St Luke's . . ."

"Mr Charles!" bellowed the Judge, "Your intervention does not assist . . . *what happened . . . is as I described . . .*"

"My Lord! Absolutely!" said Mr Charles and he sat down.

Joanne could not believe what she was hearing, she and Chris looked at each other. Things were not looking good. Or maybe Mr Charles was right. Perhaps one had to look at the whole picture. Be patient and hope that in the end Judge Sissens would make the right decision as far as Sam was concerned.

Judge Sissens continued,

"As to the future. Mr Franks is to play no further part in Sam's life, at least during Sam's childhood. He will not seek to interfere in Sam's schooling, go to the school, talk to the school, or anything of that kind. Mr Franks shall not be able to make any applications to the Court without the prior leave of the Court. There are consequences of such an Order, but" he said, "I make the Order firstly because Sam needs to be assured that this litigation is at an end. It is litigation that has been damaging to him. Secondly it will provide some assurance to the mother that the litigation is at an end and that too must be to Sam's advantage."

Judge Sissens then tackled Sam's request that a residence order should be made in favour of his mother and her husband, Dr Parry,

"I decline to make such an Order. Dr Parry has looked after Sam so far in his life and the situation is unlikely to change. Dr Parry will, I am sure, go on looking after Sam, whether or not there is a residence order."

Mr Charles then stood up and addressed Judge Sissens for the last time,

"Would Your Lordship give the mother leave to appeal?"

"No!" Judge Sissens replied emphatically. He stood up, swept his red gown behind him and abruptly left the room.

Everybody then rose to their feet, dutifully bowed and gathered up their files to leave.

Wandering outside the Court-room Joanne felt a huge relief that it was over. Gregory had at last been ordered to leave Sam alone; stop interfering in his life, particularly his school life. But inside, Joanne was still seething about the injustice of absolving Gregory of all the harm he had done to Sam's education. And what about the abuse; the way Gregory had so ill-treated Sam on visits. It was amazing how all that could be just swept away, unrecorded. To add to that, there was the huge bill from CAFCASS to pay.

"Well!" said Mr Charles cheerily to Joanne and Chris, "my best advice to you all is to take all these files, all the hundreds of bundles and *shred* them. *Shred them* and get on with your lives. Put it *all* behind you. Sam is free!"

Joanne and Chris considered his advice, but something in the back of their minds said hold on, be cautious. One day, when Joanne felt strong enough, she might need the papers to refer to. Maybe one day she would tell this story to the world.

Sometimes it can take a few years to feel secure enough to look back, when the dust has settled and see more clearly the detail, the careful choreography of how these hearings are conducted and that only what the Judges *want* to be recorded, *is* recorded. That way Court records can later be interpreted with whatever bias the Judge fancies.

When Joanne got back home Joanne hugged Sam and told him that there would be no more bad things happen; Gregory had been told to leave Sam to get on with his life.

Sam was thrilled to be free at last. He asked Joanne if he could change his name to Parry and wipe out all connection with the name Franks. Joanne got back in touch with Elizabeth and let her know the outcome of the hearing. Elizabeth was delighted and advised Joanne that since it had been declared that she was the sole parent responsible for Sam, she could do this by Deed of Change of Name. So Joanne got Sam a new passport with his new name.

Sam was so excited. He and his friends took the old passport outside onto the driveway and ritually danced and whooped around it as Sam sprayed it with his aerosol can of deodorant and set it alight. As the passport burst into flame he shouted,

"Yes! Yes! Yes! Burn! Burn! Burn!" It seemed to Sam the perfect way to rid himself of the past.

φ

Sam was accepted at a new local school. The headmistress was most impressed with Sam's determination to do well and make his way in life. He didn't have to take an entrance exam. Joanne explained that Sam had never taken an exam before, that he had had five schools in his short life and he needed a chance to prove himself. Sam proudly showed his previous schoolwork, neat and carefully laid out and with that he was told he could start in September. The headmistress was impressed with Sam's enthusiasm and said that since it was the start of a new school year, she invited Sam be the year's representative. She explained to Joanne that she hoped that it would improve his self-respect and give him a goal and a chance to show what he could do. Sam told all his friends and proudly went to see his old headmaster, Edward Williams and told him the good news. Life for Sam had taken on new meaning.

As far as CAFCASS was concerned, there was no way Chris was going to pay their bill. Out of the ten years of Court cases, CAFCASS had effectively wasted six years of Sam's life, 1998 to 2003.

Chris put together a counter claim for the cost of all the court hearings that had been caused by Miss Graves' incompetence. Interestingly, CAFCASS never responded. CAFCASS dropped their charges.

Still the fact remained that Judge Sissens had deliberately skewed his summing up of the case and that would remain in the Court files. Judge Sissens had manipulated the letter of the law like putty. He had moulded the outcome for his own (and Gregory's) end. What was more infuriating was that Judge Sissens refused to allow Joanne and Chris to appeal his judgement.

Joanne and Chris felt that Judge Sissens should not get away with this and asked Margery if they could get a second opinion from another QC.

Margery organised a meeting the following Wednesday at a the QC's chambers. The three of them arrived and were shown into a large meeting room. The QC sat at the far end of the long table, she wore a black suit and her dark hair was tied formally up into a bun, her papers and law books in front of her. She motioned to the brown leather studded chairs and invited them to take a seat round the table and help themselves to a selection of tea, coffee and biscuits. Joanne, Chris and Margery took their seats and eagerly awaited the QC's advice. She seemed to ramble on forever on this point and that and Joanne found herself getting impatient with the lack of conclusion as to how to proceed. Finally the QC gave her summing up,

"I'm sorry to say," she eventually announced, "that as far as I can see, Mr Justice Sissens left it absolutely clear that no appeal can be lodged. In other words if an application is made to appeal, it will not be allowed. I think you are stuck with the judgement. You could of course take it to the House of Lords, but that would be exceedingly expensive and I doubt that you could afford it. I will leave you a while to go over things with

Margery," and with that she shook hands with everyone and left the room.

Joanne and Chris had rather expected that would be the conclusion; that there was no redress for the suffering caused to Sam and the rest of the family through all those years of Court hearings. If a DNA test had been allowed at the beginning of the case and the Judge had acceded to the fact that Sam was born before the Act was in force, the matter could have been settled within the first year.

Margery looked thoughtfully at Joanne and Chris,

"You know there is another way of looking at all this. If you had not fought for Sam, just done nothing and left Sam living with Gregory, Sam would have been living in the most dreadful conditions. He would probably have had so little esteem for himself that he would be out on the streets, or doing drugs or theft or something. You both gave Sam a feeling of being valued, wanted and cared for and now he can go out into the world and get a good education without disruption. Although we can't change the Court records, if you wanted, there is another route. You could take your story to the newspapers and let the world know about it that way. I don't suggest that you make a decision now, but if you want to go down that route, I have a reliable journalist who would be interested."

It only took a week for Joanne and Chris to decide that telling Sam's story to the newspapers was probably the best way to expose the corruption and misreporting that went on in the Courts.

Margery arranged for Joanne and Chris to meet Harry, the journalist, in a QC's waiting room, so that there was no way that Margery could be implicated. She explained that Harry was absolutely trust-worthy; he would not let anyone else have access to any information given to him. He worked for The Sun Newspaper and that although the paper was known for sensational reporting, she had let him have other stories and he had never let her down.

Margery led Joanne and Chris to a small waiting room at the back of the main offices. It was smartly furnished with black leather low back chairs surrounding a low glass table with neatly piled newspapers and magazines. Harry sat reading a newspaper; he was a middle-aged man with greying hair, of medium build and in casual jacket and trousers. As they entered the room he stood up to greet the three of them.

"Harry!" said Margery reaching out to shake his hand, "this is Joanne and Chris; the couple I told you about."

Harry turned to greet Joanne and Chris,

"Delighted! Delighted to meet you both," he said warmly, "Margery has given me some background of the case. It's a *fascinating* story, I can't believe that this case has been allowed to go on for all these years; it's outrageous. If you are agreeable, I would be *most* interested in reporting on it."

Margery started to make her departure,

"I'll leave you all to talk now," she said and she left the room, carefully closing the door behind her.

Harry shook hands with Joanne and Chris and looked from one to the other, fascinated by the story Margery had told him,

"You really do have the most *amazing* story. I don't want to put pressure on you, or to persuade you to do anything that you do not want to do, but I promise you that you can be secure in the knowledge that your story will only be dealt with by me and my photographer, no one else. I know how to handle the story so that you are protected from being identified. Any photos will have the faces pixelated out and you will be able to approve the final version of the story before it goes to print. I do of course need enough information to make the story worth publishing, a fine line to tread, but what do you think?"

Joanne and Chris looked at each other in agreement and then Chris turned to Harry and said:

"Yes, we feel that it has to be done. The whole thing has to be exposed. What do we do next?"

"I'll come round to your house with my photographer. We'll make a few notes, take some photos, but the final decision on the text will rest with you two. Of course, because the story is about a child, Mr Murdock will have to approve the content. I'd like the story to come out as soon as possible. Would next Wednesday be a good day to meet up at your place? Sometime in the morning, say about mid-day?"

Joanne nodded,

"Yes, that would be fine, but Chris will be working at the hospital on Wednesday."

"I don't think Chris needs to be there, the story will be centered around Sam and we'd like a picture of you as his mother, but that is all. I expect the story to be on the front page, that's where it needs to be, its just such an *amazing* story! Well," he said looking excitedly at them both, "if that's all agreed, I think we best leave now. I'll see you on Wednesday." They shook hands and said their goodbyes.

Walking out of the building, holding hands Joanne and Chris felt that at last the terrible way in which this case has been handled would be out in the open, especially if it was on the front page of the newspaper.

Joanne's thoughts then turned to the advice she had been given by Margery. It would be a very risky business exposing a story such as this; she would have to be very careful when the story was published. If Joanne or Sam was recognised in the newspapers, Joanne could be accused of exposing the identity of a child and would be prosecuted—the punishment could be imprisonment. If Joanne were to be asked if it was her picture in the newspaper, she would have to dismiss the story as just another case similar to her own. Joanne had to trust that Harry and his photographer would be vigilant about every detail.

Wednesday arrived and Harry and his photographer came to the house. Joanne opened the door to the two men and she could see that they had arrived separately in two cars, one black, the other green. They were parked at the end of the drive. She led the two men into the living room and offered them coffee, but they declined, eager to get on with the job in hand. They appeared very professional, cautious and circumspect and conducted themselves in a careful and thoughtful manner. Harry and the photographer, Jim, looked about the same age. Both had short-cropped, greying hair and they seemed close friends, each knowing their role. Jim kept himself in the background, standing quietly by the window looking outside. He had a camera hanging from a strap about his neck and carried a black case with the rest of his photographic equipment. His rolled up blue shirt sleeves revealed tanned arms and his denim jeans seemed at bit at odds with his more formal black leather shoes, but, thought Joanne, if you have to walk a lot you need good strong shoes.

Harry asked Joanne to tell the story in her own words and he scribbled busily away on his note pad. Then he asked if he could see Sam on his own and hear what he had to say.

Joanne left the room and called Sam to come and speak to Harry. She felt confident that she could leave Sam alone with Harry, he seemed very caring.

After a while Harry called Joanne back into the room, then he turned to his photographer,

"Hey Jim, I think we need to make a move now,"

"Ok," said Jim, coming away from the window and then turning to Joanne he asked:

"By the way, have you got any baby photos?" Joanne shook her head, "That is so sad," said Jim, "so sad."

"You see," explained Joanne, "when Sam and I left the house I could only take what I could carry."

"Yes, I know, your solicitor filled us in with the basic details," sympathised Jim.

"Come on," said Harry earnestly, "we need to leave."

Joanne looked enquiringly at Harry. He explained:

"I don't want anyone to recognise the car. I use several different cars, but you never know who is following you, everyone wants a good story. Now I need to have some photos, but you and Sam need to change into something completely plain. I suggest a white T shirt and dark trousers, but there must be no markings either on the shirt or the trousers, nothing recognisable."

Joanne took Sam by the hand and led him up to his bedroom and selected a plain white T-shirt and navy trousers. All the trousers seemed to have some decoration on the pocket or a brand name showing, but that was all that she had. Sam changed and the two of them went back to show Harry what they had selected. Now it was Jim who was getting agitated.

"That's no good, we can't have labels showing."

"No matter," said Harry, "Sam can wear the shirt outside the trousers and hide the label." Then turning to Joanne he asked,

"How do you normally wear your hair? Is it always loose and down?"

"Usually, yes."

"Then you need to put it up,"

"Will a pony tail do?"

"Yes, if you *never* normally wear your hair in a pony tail."

Joanne quickly disappeared up to the bedroom to change into similar clothes to Sam and find a hair-band to put up her hair.

Coming back into the living room she found Harry and photographer ready to depart. Joanne looked surprised.

"We can't do the photographs here," Jim explained, "the place would be recognised. I know where we can go, come on, we need to leave now."

Joanne automatically picked up her handbag and mobile.

"No!" said Jim, "No handbags, no accessories, nothing!"

Joanne felt uneasy, but felt she had better do as she was told, however she was not going leave without her mobile and quietly slipped it into her pocket.

On the way out she grabbed the house keys and locked the door after everyone. She and Sam piled into the back seat of Harry's car and they set off following Jim's car.

Once the car had reached the main road Harry seemed to relax a little.

"Where are we going?" Joanne dared to ask, holding Sam's hand, partly as comfort for herself as much as for Sam.

"A little way further out into the country, a wooded area which is indistinguishable from any other. Don't worry we've used the place before. We have to use an area where there is no particular tree, path, wall, gate, nothing anyone could recognise; just general foliage."

The next forty minutes seemed an age. Joanne did not recognise the route they were being taken and she felt vulnerable. She nervously felt for her mobile in her pocket to reassure herself that it was still there. It was a hot sunny day and it could have been a pleasant drive, but the atmosphere in the car was still tense. Sam sat obediently beside her, he seemed quite at ease with it all.

At last Jim turned off the road into a lane and after going a short way, pulled his car to the side and stopped. Harry followed and parked behind him. Looking out of the window Joanne could see a pleasant leafy wood on either side of the lane, with tiny narrow paths going here and there, but mostly everything looked over-grown, as though it was not often used.

"We'll get out here, " said Harry, "follow Jim."

Joanne and Sam got out of the car and followed Jim up a small path. Joanne led Sam by the hand, dodging low branches and pushing aside the ferns and nettles with her feet as she went, paving the way for Sam behind her. She was glad she was wearing trousers to protect her legs, but it was hot and the sun beat down uncomfortably on her neck.

After a while Jim stopped.

"Here will do," he said, "I want you both to stop here. I'm going a little further on. I want you both to turn your backs to me as though you are walking away from me and I want you, Joanne, to put your arm around Sam."

Joanne did as she was told. It was difficult for her and Sam to be both on the path at the same time, it was too narrow, so she stood in the long grass at the side and allowed Sam space on the path.

"I'll have to stand here in the long grass," Joanne called back over her shoulder.

"That doesn't matter," said Jim, "I don't want to show your feet in the picture, footwear can easily be recognised. I'll only be taking a picture of the back of your heads to just below your knees."

Obediently Joanne and Sam stood there in the sun while Jim took photographs from various angles. Sometimes they had to walk on in front of him, sometimes they were asked to turn slightly towards each other.

"Ok. I think that's enough. Now I need a close-up picture of Sam."

Sam looked up anxiously at Joanne. As Jim came towards them he noticed Sam's worried expression.

"Don't worry, the faces will be pixellated-out. No one will be able to recognise you. It's just that we need some outline features. Afterwards the pictures will all be destroyed."

Harry was watching them from a couple of yards away. He had found himself a leafy tree to stand under. He motioned to Joanne to join him and leave Jim to photograph Sam. Joanne walked towards him, glad of the shade.

Harry was talking quietly, almost as though he was talking to himself.

"It was both fascinating and sad to listen to what Sam had to say."

Joanne looked at Harry's face. He seemed a kind man, not like the aggressive types that you sometimes read about.

He continued:

"Sam said he *knew* that there was something strange about the man that everyone called his father. He said that he had listened to his friends talk about their fathers and they had said that they all had similar interests to their dads, or looked like their dads, or there was something to make them feel bonded. But Sam said he didn't look anything like Gregory Franks, he didn't have the same hair, the same eyes, nothing. He didn't have similar interests or share the same likes or dislikes and that Mr Franks was a hard man, aggressive and sometimes even cruel. He seemed to enjoy criticising Sam and apparently called him dyslexic and all sorts of names."

Joanne listened to Harry in surprise. She hadn't realised that Sam had been so observant or had discussed the matter with his friends. So Sam had *instinctively* felt that there was no connection between himself and Gregory Franks. It was interesting that children could feel a natural bond, or not, as the case may be.

Harry went on,

"Sam seems a gentle, sensitive boy, kind and aware of other people's feelings. He told me he couldn't understand the Judge, because although the Judge had apparently said that he wanted to do the best for Sam, the Judge never seemed to listen to anything Sam said.

Or, maybe it was the welfare officer who never told the Judge what Sam said. Either way, Sam said he had spent all his childhood going through assessments, interviews and Court hearings and he wanted his life back. He said Mr Franks owes him his life back. That now no one is going to tell him how to live his life anymore, it's his life and he is the one who's got to live it." Harry paused and then commented, " Sam is very mature for his age."

Joanne nodded, she felt sad that her little son had been through so much and that she had been unable to protect him from Judge Sissens's relentless determination to make him have contact with a man whom he did not like and who treated him cruelly. Joanne and Chris had stood by Sam throughout the ordeal and it had been exhausting. They had spent all their weekends preparing documents for Court, statement after statement and they had spent every penny that they could lay their hands on to afford solicitors to advise them.

Ten years of being hounded by Mr Franks in collusion with the Judges and the welfare officers. Eighty Court hearings. Sam's little brother, Alex, had suffered too. Alex was too young to understand why his parents spent all weekend working, getting papers ready for Court, but during that time he had been deprived of his parent's attention.

Well, it was all over now. Perhaps now at last they could live a normal life.

Jim finished taking the photographs of Sam and brought him back to Joanne.

"That's good. Thank you. Now we need to get you both back home. I think its best you come in my car this time. We will send you a copy of the photos and what we feel is appropriate to write so that you can comment on the content before it goes to print." He led the way back to where they had parked the cars and Harry drove back to work, while Jim turned his car around and drove Joanne and Sam back home.

Chris and Alex were waiting for them as they entered the house, Springer's tail wagging as he bounded around them with excitement. Chris put his arms around Joanne and Sam and little Alex in the middle flung his arms around Joanne and squeezed her tight.

"Family hug," laughed Chris, relieved to have everyone back home again.

Chapter Eleven

Back to Barcelona

Joanne woke with a start. It must have been Chris's arms around her, giving her an extra squeeze that made her wake up. Gosh! She must have slept through most of the movie. Joanne rubbed her eyes and tried to focus on the TV screen. Chris would tease her if he knew she'd been asleep. She knew North Country was quite a long film, so maybe she could pick up the story from when she had gone to sleep.

Joanne watched the girl on the screen as she tried to explain to her son why she had decided to speak up about how badly the men treated the women in the mines. She had dared to speak out, to protect the other women working there and that was what had started the furore.

Joanne could see herself in a similar situation, explaining to Sam why she had to expose the bias of the Courts; their bias to one of their barristers and how easily CAFCASS had been coerced into following a certain course, instead of being independent.

CAFCASS had let Sam down; they had put the wishes of adults before the wishes of the child, in particular the wishes of the barrister involved and the Judge had collaborated with him.

Joanne sighed and promised herself that one day she would write a book about Sam and maybe they would make a movie of it too.

She curled her body around Chris, enjoying the feeling of warmth and security that he gave her. She knew how lucky she was to have his love and support and how lucky Sam and Alex were to have such a wonderful father and she loved him with all her heart.

Chapter Twelve

Today

It was three years later; a day like any other Spring day. The 'phone rang and Joanne picked up the receiver. A formal voice came down the line,

"Mrs Parry?"

"Yes. Speaking!"

"Mrs Parry, its Mrs Keene the deputy head from Sam's school. Sam is fine, nothing to worry about. However, I thought you should know that we received a visit at lunchtime today from Mr Franks, demanding to see Sam. Of course we have the Court Order and we know where we stand. The staff called security to reception and Mr Franks was politely asked to leave. I'm not sure what you want to do about this. It maybe that Mr Franks will not approach the school again, although I have to warn you that, in our experience, people like Mr Franks may obey a Court Order for a while but then lapse back into their old ways! We decided not to tell Sam so as not to unsettle him . . ."

φ

Sam packed his books into his knapsack, it was the end of another school day. He looked out of the classroom window, screwing his eyes up against the bright afternoon sunshine. It looked to be warm enough, he thought and stuffed his hoody in with his books before slinging the bag over his shoulder.

Outside in the sunshine he breathed a big sigh of relief, not too much homework tonight and began to stroll leisurely down the road. Maybe he'd get a coffee and bun from Starbucks before setting off for home.

Then he felt the hairs on the back of his neck start to stand up. Creepy, he thought, that feels really weird, but he decided that it was not going to bother him and he ignored it. But the feeling would not go away. Sam felt that someone was watching him, someone behind him. What was it, he thought, that made you aware that someone was staring at you? Crazy stuff and he scrunched his shoulders high up to his neck to try and get rid of the feeling. He certainly wasn't going to give whoever it was the satisfaction of him turning round to see who it was. Then Sam was aware of the soft purr of an engine coming slowly behind him. Someone was following him. He could feel the car creeping along some yards behind. Sam shrugged; so someone was looking for somewhere to park or something? But something made him lengthen his stride. He could hear the vehicle getting closer, crawling along and he imagined he could almost feel the heat of the engine as it closed in on him. Sam saw a narrow alleyway on his left, too narrow for a car and decided to turn into it. He didn't know where it led, but so what! The wheels of the car slowed to a halt at the entrance to the alleyway. The driver watched Sam disappear from view, then leant back in his seat as a wry smile spread over his face.

φ

The harassment carried on for a while. Sam received letters, but he sent them back without opening

192

them. He really was finished with all of that. Gradually he began to grow into a normal life, but his childhood was gone; taken by a vindictive man who was able to manipulate an unfit system and it had left its mark.